The Sun Shines
A Collection of Nature Literature

The Sun Shines
A Collection of Nature Literature

Edited with an Introduction by Kimberly Paulo

WHITLOCK PUBLISHING
Alfred, NY

First Whitlock Publishing Edition 2025
Whitlock Publishing
Alfred, New York
http://www.whitlockpublishing.com

ISBN: 978-1-943115-59-4

This book was set in Adobe Garamond on 50# acid-free paper that meets ANSI standards for archival quality.

For my family and friends.

Table of Contents

Introduction i
Timeline of Nature Literature and Historical Contexts viii
British Authors
William Shakespeare 1
Sonnets
11 3
18 4
20 5
67 6
68 7
Gilbert White 9
The Invitation to Selborne 11
A Harvest Scene 15
John Keats 17
Ode to a Nightingale 19
To Autumn 22
Elizabeth Barrett Browning 25
Patience Taught by Nature 29
The Deserted Garden 30
American Authors
Ralph Waldo Emerson 35
Nature
Introduction 39
Chapter I: Nature 41
Chapter II: Commodity 45
Chapter III: Beauty 47
Chapter IV: Language 53
Chapter V: Discipline 59
Chapter VI: Idealism 65

Chapter VII: Spirit 73
Chapter VIII: Prospects 77
Henry David Thoreau 85
Walden
Chapter II: Where I Lived... 89
Chapter XV: Winter Animals 103
Chapter XVI: The Pond in Winter 113
Chapter XVII: Spring 125
Conclusion 141
Anne Spencer 153
Lines to a Nasturtium 157
White Things 158
Life-Long, Poor Browning... 159
Suggested Reading 161
Bibliography 163

Introduction

"The sun shines today also."

—Ralph Waldo Emerson, *Nature.*

Have you ever questioned the importance of nature? Are you scared of aging and losing your childhood? Do you fear the inevitability of death? So did Shakespeare! While you may not write 154 sonnets to cope with the thought of never leaving your mark on history, other authors use their writing to express the beauty that Earth creates through nature. All people eventually die, but nature persists. Nature inspires writers to look forward to the sun rising the next day rather than worrying about the hardships of war, racism, mortality, and self-purpose.

From flora to fauna, every part of nature impacts how humans tackle tough situations. Nature is Earth's art. Themes of exploring the world around us in nature literature allow readers to watch how authors navigate the natural world through writing. To some, nature is hard and unforgiving because of its frosty winters. To others, nature represents perseverance and rebirth through spring. By bridging the gap between nature and readers, literature shapes how people personally define nature.

Many of the works here, including John Keats' "Ode to a Nightingale" (1819) and Ralph Waldo Emerson's *Nature* (1836), focus on the eighteenth-century aesthetic theory of the "sublime." The sublime can represent anything in culture and speaks to one's experience beyond aesthetics. It reaches magnitudes that can exceed human thought by representing powerful scenes of nature that inspire a sense of awe. The sublime cannot be like nature, but nature can be extraordinary enough to be sublime. The sublime is ineffable and frightening at times, but its mysteriousness inspires writers to explore.

While readers imagine the natural spaces described by nature writers, nature also plays its role in connecting with human culture. The philosophy behind landscapes differs across regions. North America often embraces the unknown, untamed wilderness of the new nation while Europeans were more diverse in their thoughts about nature. Some Europeans feared the wild due to plague outbreaks and vicious animals, while some thought of nature as tame land for pastoral writings. Despite the regional differences, human life intertwines with the environment. Without the environment, humanity would struggle. Nature promotes mindfulness and curiosity for future generations because people place those beliefs onto nature. The writers included in this anthology use their nature literature to share their own experience with the outdoors and how it connects to their experiences.

The British View on Nature

Few landscapes have been impacted by human activity more than the British Isles. British culture passes down through people leaving their marks on nature, which is apparent through literature dating back to the seventeenth century. Specifically, the Lake District, later becoming the first British national park, is known for its presence in literature for its wildness and beauty. Despite this, Lake District is hardly "natural," as its wilderness is primarily human made. The district's carefully crafted beauty reflects the British's fear of unfamiliar, true wilderness. Romantic poets such as Samuel Taylor Coleridge and William Wordsworth drew inspiration from the Lake District's scenery. Wordsworth's "I Wandered Lonely as a Cloud" (1807) captured the region's beauty and Beatrix Potter based the setting of "The Tale of Peter Rabbit" (1902) on the landscape.

Nature reflects human experience. Many early Europeans saw nature as terrifying. To them, nature produced sharp-toothed animals, mountains that covered the horizon, and storms that killed people without warning. Natural areas in Europe had to either be manmade, like the Lake District, or carefully protected from the deforestation and draining bogs that came with the industrializing of Europe. Writers became inspired by the aesthetics of the Lake

District, the Alps, and other natural scenes—all glimpses of the sublime. For example, Lord Byron's "Childe Harold's Pilgrimage" (1812) exhibits the excitement of nature compared to man. Nature literature slowly made nature something to admire, rather than something to fear.

The Eighteenth Century and Naturalists

Poetry and art prospered from nature's impact on man, eventually leading to the beginning of the first Romantic generation that lasted until the nineteenth century. Not only did Romantic poetry gain popularity, but experts of natural history, known as naturalists, were on the rise with new ways to study nature. New tools for collecting nature, such as butterfly nets and geological hammers, became more prominent. Nature-collecting equipment developed quickly, and the use of the tools allowed for better models to be invented through trial and error, such as cultivating forks aiding field research. Botanists thrived with the new ways to gather species to study. Specifically, Sébastien Vaillant and Rudolph Jacob Camerarius, a French and German botanist respectively, both studied sex reproduction between plants that aided in Carl Linnaeus' idea that all organisms reproduce sexually (along with a huge collection containing thousands of specimens). Linnaeus then created the binomial nomenclature, a way to name the discovered flora and fauna.

Most naturalists kept many tools on hand to be prepared for any type of land exploration. With improved technology, people were able to make new discoveries in nature, causing a boom in travel journals and informational texts. Gilbert White's *The Natural History and Antiquities of Selborne* (1789) included letters to Thomas Pennant and Daines Barrington, other naturalists. The letters included observations of different animals, plants, and his discovery of the harvest mouse with its mostly vegetarian diet of seeds, roots, and fruit. Learning about how different species work helps other naturalists learn how to preserve nature while still being able to collect materials needed for study. The early efforts of the eighteenth-century naturalists, like Linnaeus and White, paved the way for Charles Darwin's evolution theory that species change and adapt over time to new environments. Darwin's theory further supports that nature is controlled in transformed (through the scientific process) in Great Britain unlike the often-carefree American ideas on wilderness.

British Romanticism

The Romantic period introduced more writing that emphasized the individual and imagination. With Romanticism at its peak in the early 1800s, works often focused on the celebration of nature, as many writers used nature as inspiration and felt connected with nature spiritually. Many Romantic poets had an appreciation for the beauty of nature and distaste for the growing urbanization of their country. Industrialization promoted the loss of natural landscape but was also the start of the increased class differences between the growing impoverished and rich. Urbanity motivated Romanticists to explore their own feelings and see nature as a source of inspiration. Coleridge's poem, "To Nature" (1796), expresses his love for the outdoors and the joy it gives him. John Clare used his poem "The Lament of Swordy Well" to write from the point of view of the land and the effect that large scale farming and industrialization had on it.

The sublime was even more prominent in Romantic writing, as not only was it a source of awe, but also of fear since the notion of the sublime is not something a writer could grasp. Percy Bysshe Shelley, a second-generation Romantic writer, uses "Mont Blanc" (1817) to show that the human imagination cannot comprehend something as grand as the Alps. Ann Radcliffe bases *The Mysteries of Udolpho* (1794) and *The Italian* (1796) on sublime landscapes as well. With so many unknowns in the world, the previous teachings of naturalists, and the Romantics' urge to understand nature gave readers the desire to preserve, clean, and overall be closer to nature for a chance to even experience the sublime.

The Romantics would continue to inspire Victorian period writers, such as Elizabeth Barrett Browning. While the majority of Barrett Browning's literature was produced in the Victorian era, a period that saw the rise of novels, industrialization, and literacy rates, her works often focused on individual experience. "The Deserted Garden"

(1838) reflects the childlike wonder that is lost once one grows up but reignites that curiosity once the narrator explores an abandoned garden—discovering something that was once lost.

The American View on Nature

Having a newly discovered nation changed how wild landscapes were perceived, so American writers wished to separate their works from the contemporary British literature to make something uniquely American. The undomesticated lands motivated writers to explore new territories, and what Americans saw were thriving ecosystems, relatively untouched by man. Nature writing increased one's identification with one's own nation by writing about the beauties that their new nation offered. The Transcendentalists, like Ralph Waldo Emerson and David Henry Thoreau, who valued insight rather than opinions of others, were the most influential for nationalism through their works about how one can live off nature self-reliantly, like growing your own food.

America and Great Britain started to have similar ideas about nature—it is based on human experience. The difference come in how each region, as British writers often drew inspiration from jaw dropping landscapes, Americans used the birth of the nation to grow their understanding on the new land. At the end of the American Civil War, with inspiration from the British Romantic movement, literature became more distinctly American. Henry Wadsworth Longfellow helped cultivate the American Renaissance with poems like "The Song of Hiawatha" (1855) and "Paul Revere's Ride" (1860), both using American events as inspiration. His poem, "Nature" (1878), compares nature to the loving affection of a mother guiding her son through life. Another leading member of the American Renaissance, James Russell Lowell, had influence from Wordsworth and Coleridge to emphasize the power of the natural world and imagination within his poetry. Lowell's "The First Snowfall" (1855) uses nature to act as a healing agent for a loss and loneliness. Even though nature is not sentient and has no emotions, Lowell promotes human connection to nature because nature, to him, has transformative power and heals.

Transcendentalism

Many New England philosophers valued insight rather than history to reveal truths, starting the American Transcendentalism movement. Transcendentalism is based on one's own experience, so the definitions may vary, but having such a loose definition is more appropriate for the movement. Typically, transcendentalists thought that people are innately good that they should turn to in times of decision instead of basing decisions on social expectations and lessons from history being completely self-reliant.

In a time when the new American nation is expanding West and the battle for equal rights between sexes and races grew, being able to rely on oneself rather than the decisions of others seemed appealing. The carefree nature of Transcendentalism inspired all writers, but inspiration seldom came from other authors, as the movement values individuality and self-expression. The only way to gain insight was to gather information without the help of others. Henry David Thoreau in *Walden* (1854) chose solitude in nature to discover himself along with exploring the natural wilderness that the new nation provided. Ralph Waldo Emerson, one of the most popular American Transcendentalists, used his essay, *Nature* (1836), to reflect on the power of nature and how it acts as a source of enlightenment.

Harlem Renaissance

With the growing nation modernizing through the twentieth century, it shifted its focus to the equality between all men. Despite the abolishment of slavery, African Americans still did not receive the same rights as white people. While the fight for equality among races continued, a step toward progress was in the 1920s with the creative movement, the Harlem Renaissance. The movement highlighted Black artists who used their talents to voice African American struggles.

Since World War I called upon minorities to fight in the front lines, once the war concluded, many relocated to New York City. As the city's population grew, Harlem especially had a boom in population, becoming the largest African American community in the United States. The rise in citizens caused an increase in the arts, as many Harlem residents pursued higher education.

With the burst of creativity and intellect in Harlem, Black authors started to use their knowledge to write about the continuously bad treatment of Black Americans. W.E.B. Du Bois started editing *The Crisis*, a journal put out by the National Association for the Advancement of Colored People (NAACP), that highlighted Black authors of the movement and reflected the African American experience. Jessie R. Fauset also edited The Crisis published "Rondeau" (1912) about looking forward to the rebirth of life in spring and Langston Hughes depicted the African American experience through his works and mentions spring's arrival in "An Earth Song" (1917). Writers often used natural themes because comparing African American hardships to nature helped make the literature more accessible to non-Black Americans.

Timeline of Nature Literature and Historical Contexts

1604 The first English dictionary published; *A Table Alphabetical.*
1608 Major bubonic plague outbreak causes theaters to close.
1609 William Shakespeare, "Sonnets"
1634 The first English settlers arrive in Maryland.
1642 Banning of public theatres by English parliament.
1660 Charles II reopens public theatres after becoming King.
1726 The start of the Great Awakening increased interest in Christianity, thus increasing literature with religious themes.
1776 The signing of The Declaration of Independence.
1789 Gilbert White, *The Natural History of Selborne*
1798 William Wordsworth and Samuel Taylor Coleridge have "Lyrical Ballads" published, marking the approximate start of the English Romantic movement.
1803 Louisiana Purchase, indicating the start of the American westward expansion and more exploration of American landscapes.
1804 Lewis and Clark set off on their expedition to scout a route across the American West • Inspired by a walking tour and daffodils, William Wordsworth writes "I Wandered Lonely as a Cloud"
1816 The beginning of economic suffering in Europe due to Napoleonic Wars.
1819 John Keats, "Odes"
1827 A group of Black citizens, including Samuel Cornish, a Presbyterian minister, and John Brown Russwurm, one of the first African Americans to graduate from a U.S. college, create *Freedom's Journal*, the first African American owned and operated newspaper.

1830 The Church of Christ of Latter-Day Saints is established.

~1830s The want for distinctly American literary works increased thus beginning the American Renaissance in which American literature was an expression of national spirit.

1831 William Lloyd Garrison publishes the antislavery journal, *The Liberator.*

1836 Ralph Waldo Emerson, *Nature* • Narcissa Prentiss Whitman sends letters and journal entries to relatives describing the beauties of the West while on the Oregon Trail, motivating others to make the journey.

1837 Queen Victoria begins her reign, marking the start of the Victorian Era • Ralph Waldo Emerson delivers his "The American Scholar" speech which urged Americans to look to themselves and American landscapes for inspiration rather than Europe.

1840 Elizabeth Barrett Browning, "The Deserted Garden"

1841 Ralph Waldo Emerson publishes "Self-Reliance," an essay advocating about trusting one's own thoughts and promoting individualism.

1845 Elizabeth Barrett Browning, "Patience Taught by Nature" • Henry David Thoreau, *Walden.*

1861 American Civil War breaks out between the North and the South over whether all men were created with an equal right to liberty.

1865 Thirteenth Amendment abolishes slavery in the United States.

1866 The Civil Rights Act bans discrimination based on race, religion, or color.

1910 A group of Black citizens publish *The Crisis*, the official NAACP magazine that brings racial inequality to light, with W.E.B. Du Bois as one of the editors.

1917 Langston Hughes publishes "An Earth Song."

~1920s The Harlem Renaissance is at its peak, promoting art, literature, and music from Black artists.

1923 Anne Spencer, "White Things"

1926 Anne Spencer, "Lines to a Nasturtium"

1927 Anne Spencer, "Life-Long, Poor Browning…"

William Shakespeare (1564–1616)

Though his exact birth date is unknown, William Shakespeare was born around April 23rd in 1564. In his hometown, Stratford-upon-Avon, he was baptized on April 26th. He was one of eight children, although his two older sisters did not survive infancy. His father, John Shakespeare, worked as a craftsman while his mother, Mary Arden, was the daughter of a wealthy family and was left a large piece of land after the death of her father. At eighteen, Shakespeare married twenty-six-year-old Anne Hathaway, who was already pregnant with their first daughter, Susanna. Shortly after, Hathaway gave birth to their twins, Hamnet and Judith. Hamnet died at just eleven years old, but Shakespeare's two other children reached adulthood.

Many of Shakespeare's later works had Greek and Roman themes thanks to his education. Along with his brothers, Shakespeare attended a grammar school where he learned Latin and Greek. By 1594, Shakespeare was already an established poet in London and had written Richard III and The Taming of the Shrew. It was then when he joined The Lord Chamberlain's Men, a company of actors where Shakespeare worked as a both an actor and a playwright. During this time, he wrote many of his most famous plays, including King Lear, Macbeth, Romeo and Juliet, and A Midsummer Night's Dream.

In 1609, Shakespeare's famous sonnets were published. This collection of 154 poems explores themes of love, mortality, nature, beauty, and time. The first seventeen sonnets later became known as the 'procreation sonnets,' for they urge a young man to immortalize his beauty by passing it on to his children, as age will diminish the beauty of man and nature.

William Shakespeare died in 1616, but his influence on literature has never waned. Many English phrases used today have come from his plays, such as "wear your heart on your sleeve" and "heart of gold." His plays are regularly performed in theatres around the world, and Sonnet 116 is frequently read at wedding ceremonies.

— 11 —

As fast as thou shalt wane, so fast thou growest
In one of thine, from that which thou departest;
And that fresh blood which youngly thou bestowest
Thou mayst call thine when thou from youth convertest.
Herein lives wisdom, beauty and increase:
Without this, folly, age and cold decay:
If all were minded so, the times should cease
And threescore year would make the world away.
Let those whom Nature hath not made for store,
Harsh featureless and rude, barrenly perish:
Look, whom she best endow'd she gave the more;
Which bounteous gift thou shouldst in bounty cherish:
    She carved thee for her seal, and meant thereby
    Thou shouldst print more, not let that copy die.

— 18 —

Shall I compare thee to a summer's day?
Thou art more lovely and more temperate:
Rough winds do shake the darling buds of May,
And summer's lease hath all too short a date;
Sometime too hot the eye of heaven shines,
And often is his gold complexion dimm'd;
And every fair from fair sometime declines,
By chance or nature's changing course untrimm'd;
But thy eternal summer shall not fade,
Nor lose possession of that fair thou ow'st;
Nor shall death brag thou wander'st in his shade,
When in eternal lines to time thou grow'st:
So long as men can breathe or eyes can see,
So long lives this, and this gives life to thee.

— 20 —

A woman's face with nature's own hand painted
Hast thou, the master-mistress of my passion;
A woman's gentle heart, but not acquainted
With shifting change as is false women's fashion;
An eye more bright than theirs, less false in rolling,
Gilding the object whereupon it gazeth;
A man in hue, all hues in his controlling,
Which steals men's eyes and women's souls amazeth.
And for a woman wert thou first created,
Till nature as she wrought thee fell a-doting,
And by addition me of thee defeated
By adding one thing to my purpose nothing.
    But since she pricked thee out for women›s pleasure,
    Mine be thy love and thy love's use their treasure.

— 67 —

Ah! wherefore with infection should he live,
And with his presence grace impiety,
That sin by him advantage should achieve,
And lace itself with his society?
Why should false painting imitate his cheek,
And steal dead seeming of his living hue?
Why should poor beauty indirectly seek
Roses of shadow, since his rose is true?
Why should he live, now Nature bankrupt is,
Beggared of blood to blush through lively veins?
For she hath no exchequer now but his,
And proud of many, lives upon his gains.
    O! him she stores, to show what wealth she had
    In days long since, before these last so bad.

— 68 —

Thus is his cheek the map of days outworn,
When beauty lived and died as flowers do now,
Before these bastard signs of fair were born,
Or durst inhabit on a living brow;
Before the golden tresses of the dead,
The right of sepulchres, were shorn away,
To live a second life on second head;
Ere beauty's dead fleece made another gay:
In him those holy antique hours are seen,
Without all ornament, itself and true,
Making no summer of another's green,
Robbing no old to dress his beauty new;
    And him as for a map doth Nature store,
    To show false Art what beauty was of yore.

GILBERT WHITE (1720–93)

REVEREND GILBERT WHITE, AN ENGLISH NATURALIST, was born July 20th, 1720. He was one of eleven children to John White, a barrister, and Anne Holt. White spent almost all his time in or around his hometown of Selborne in Hampshire, England. He eventually enrolled at Oriel College in the University of Oxford where he got his Bachelor of Arts in 1743, a fellowship in 1744, and his Master of Arts in 1746. That same year, White got his deacon's orders, and three years later he was fully ordained.

Soon after his ordination, White began writing journals in which he noted the changes in his garden. In 1765, he released his findings in a Calendar of Flora and the Garden. Despite being a fellow at Oxford still, White spent most of his later life studying more flora, animals, and landscapes in Selbourne. In 1767, White began his observations of the smallest European mouse, the harvest mouse. He first noticed that the two-inch mouse closes the hole to its nest whenever it leaves and enters, like a door. These observations, along with other notes about its nests consisting of corn and thistles, are seen in letters White wrote to Thomas Pennant, a Welsh naturalist. Letters like these eventually made their way into White's most famous work, *The Natural History of Selborne* (1789), a work that has not been out of print since its first publication.

White fully moved back to Selborne in 1755 after the death of his father, but it was not until the death of his uncle in 1763 that White inherited his childhood home, The Wakes. Selbourne became the main source of inspiration for White's letters to acquaintances that later were formalized (or completely changed literary styles) for the basis for his book. In 1780, White suffered the death of his aunt Rebecca Snooke, causing him to inherit her pet tortoise, Timothy. Timothy was in many of White's accounts in *The Natural History of Selborne.* The tortoise was also the inspiration of Verlyn Klinkenborg's book, *Timothy; or, Notes of an Abject Reptile* (2006).

Following his death on June 26th, 1793, White was buried at St. Mary's Church in Selbourne where his simple gravestone is marked with the initials 'GW.' In 1920, the church installed a stained-glass window memorializing him. In 1955, his home became the Gilbert White Museum, a place where visitors can learn about White and scholars can find many of his manyscripts.

The Invitation to Selborne

See Selborne spreads her boldest beauties round
The varied valley, and the mountain ground,
Wildly majestic! what is all the pride
Of flats, with loads of ornament supply'd?
Unpleasing, tasteless, impotent expense,
Compar'd with nature's rude magnificence.
 Arise, my stranger, to these wild scenes haste
The unfinish'd farm awaits your forming taste:
Plan the pavilion, airy, light and true;
Thro' the high arch call in the lengthening view;
Expand the forest sloping up the hill;
Swell to a lake the scant, penurious rill;
Extend the vista, raise the castle mound
In antique taste, with turrets ivy-crown'd;
O'er the gay lawn the flow'ry shrub dispread,
Or with the blending garden mix the mead;
Bid China's pale, fantastic fence, delight,
Or with the mimic statue trap the sight.
 Oft on some evening, sunny, soft and still,
The Muse shall lead thee to the beech-grown hill,
To spend in tea the cool, refreshing hour,
Where nods in air the pensile, nest-like bower;
Or where the Hermit hangs the straw-clad cell,
Emerging gently from the leafy dell;
By fancy plann'd; as once th' inventive maid
Met the boar sage amid the secret shade;
Romantic spot! from whence in prospect lies
Whate'er of landscape charms our feasting eyes;
The pointed spire, the hall, the pasture-plain,

The russet fallow, or the golden grain,
The breezy lake that sheds a gleaming light,
Till all the fading picture fail the sight.
Each to his task; all different ways retire,
Cull the dry stick; call forth the seeds of fire;
Deep fix the kettle's props, a forky row,
Or give with fanning bat the breeze to blow.
Whence is this taste, the furnish'd hall forgot,
To feast in gardens, or th'unhandy grot?
Or novelty with some new charms surprises,
Or from our very shifts some joy arises.
Hark, while below the village-bells ring round,
Echo, sweet nymph, returns the soften'd sound;
But if gusts rise, the rushing forests roar,
Like the tide tumbling on the pebbly shore.
Adown the vale, in lone, sequester'd nook,
Where skirting woods imbrown the dimpling brook,
The ruin'd Convent lies; here wont to dwell
The lazy canon midst his cloistered cell;
While papal darkness brooded o'er the land,
Ere reformation made her glorious stand:
Still oft at eve belated shepherd-swains
See the cowl'd spectre skim the folded plains.
To the high temple would my stranger go,
The mountain-brow commands the woods below;
In Jewry first this order found a name,
When madding Croisades set the world in flame;
When western climes, urg'd on by Pope and priest,
Pour'd forth their millions o'er the deluged east;
Luxurious knights, ill suited to defy
To mortal fight Turcéstan chivalry.
Nor be the Parsonage by the muse forgot.
The partial bard admires his native spot;
Smit with its beauties, loved, as yet a child,
(Unconscious why) its scapes grotesque, and wild.
High on a mound th' exalted gardens stand,
Beneath, deep vallies scoop'd by nature's hand.

A Cobham here, exulting in his art,
Might blend the General's with the Gardener's part;
Might fortify with all the martial trade
Of rampart, bastion, fosse, and palisade;
Might plant the mortar with wide threatening bore,
Or bid the mimic cannon seem to roar.
Now climb the steep, drop now your eye below,
Where round the blooming village orchards grow;
There, like a picture, lies my lowly seat,
A rural, shelter'd, unobserved retreat.
Me far above the rest Selbornian scenes,
The pendent forests, and the mountain-greens
Strike with delight; there spreads the distant view,
That gradual fades till sunk in misty blue:
Here nature hangs her slopy woods to sight,
Rills purl between and dart a quivering light.

A Harvest Scene

Wak'd by the gentle gleamings of the morn,
Soon clad, the reaper, provident of want
Hies cheerful hearted to the ripen'd field;
Nor hastes alone; attendant by his side
His faithful wife, sole partner of his cares,
Bears on her breast the sleeping babe; behind
With steps unequal trips her infant train:
Thrice happy pair, in love and labour join'd! —
All day they ply their task; with mutual chat
Beguiling each the sultry, tedious hours:
Around them falls in rows the sever'd corn,
Or the shocks rise in regular array.
But when high noon invites to short repast
Beneath the shade of sheltering thorn they sit,
Divide the simple meal, and drain the cask:
The swinging cradle lulls the whimpering babe,
Meantime; while growling round, if at the tread
Of hasty passenger alarm'd, as of their store
Protective, stalks the cur with bristling back,
To guard the scanty scrip and russet frock.

John Keats (1795–1821)

In London, England, John Keats was born on October 31st in 1795. Living only to the age of twenty-five, Keats devoted his life to creating vivid imagery through his poetry. Keats had fifty-four poems published before his premature death. Despite this, many readers consider Keats to be one of the most talented of the second wave of Romantic poets, a group that includes Lord Byron and Percy Bysshe Shelley.

Being the oldest of five children, Keats seemingly had a loving childhood and was close with his siblings. His father, Thomas Keats, was a stable manager who fell in love and married his employer's daughter, Frances Jennings. After the death of Keats' father in 1804, Frances remarried soon after. However, the new couple separated and all the Keats children moved in with their grandmother in Edmonton.

Just two miles away, Keats attended John Clarke's school in Enfield where his literary aspirations began to take shape. By 1809, Keats was an avid reader, but he still did not end up devoting his life to poetry until 1816. During those seven years, Keats apprenticed as a surgeon at sixteen but broke off his apprenticeship to live in London. There, Keats worked at hospitals as a junior house surgeon.

Keats still had literature on his mind and spent the rest of his life on writing poetry. Charles Cowden Clarke, the son of John Clarke, was the catalyst for Keats' interest in poetry. Young Clarke introduced Keats to Edmund Spenser and Elizabethan literature, both becoming models for his earliest works. Also inspired by George Chapman's seventeenth century translation of the *Iliad* and the *Odyssey*, Keats wrote his first mature sonnet, "On First Looking into Chapman's Homer" (1816). In Keats' first long poems, *Endymion* (1817), he transformed the Greek legend of the love between the moon goddess and Endymion, a mortal shepherd. Keats focused on the romantic theme of the poem through grand adventures with sensuous descriptions. Despite the poem being 4,000 lines long, Keats still seemed dissatisfied with it. During a brief trip to the Lake District in northern England, Keats developed his first symptoms of tuberculosis. Upon his return to London, he was met with brutal criticism of *Endymion* in the *Quarterly Review*. Despite the critics, Keats calmly continued to write poetry.

In 1818, Keats fell in love with Fannie Brawne, his neighbor in Hampstead. While their relationship could not run its course because of Keats' sickness, the two become engaged in October 1819. It was during this year that Keats wrote his greatest poetry, including his great odes, such as "Ode on a Grecian Urn," "Ode to a Nightingale," and "To Autumn." His budding relationship and strain of his deteriorating health inspired these poems. The odes reflect Keats' philosophy of the imagination as a bridge between his inner being and the natural world around him.

Near the end of his life, Keats' wrote other poems such as "The Eve of St. Agnes" and "Isabella." By 1820, his tuberculosis diagnosis was clear and sustained work became impossible. Keats sailed to Italy for a different climate in hopes of getting well enough to return and marry Fanny, but in February 1821, he died in Rome. Keats' reputation in the nineteenth century continued to grow after his death, influencing poets like Alfred, Lord Tennyson.

Ode to a Nightingale

My heart aches, and a drowsy numbness pains
My sense, as though of hemlock I had drunk,
Or emptied some dull opiate to the drains
One minute past, and Lethe-wards had sunk:
'Tis not through envy of thy happy lot,
But being too happy in thine happiness, —
That thou, light-winged Dryad of the trees
In some melodious plot
Of beechen green, and shadows numberless,
Singest of summer in full-throated ease.

O, for a draught of vintage! that hath been
Cool'd a long age in the deep-delved earth,
Tasting of Flora and the country green,
Dance, and Provençal song, and sunburnt mirth!
O for a beaker full of the warm South,
Full of the true, the blushful Hippocrene,
With beaded bubbles winking at the brim,
And purple-stained mouth;
That I might drink, and leave the world unseen,
And with thee fade away into the forest dim:

Fade far away, dissolve, and quite forget
What thou among the leaves hast never known,
The weariness, the fever, and the fret
Here, where men sit and hear each other groan;
Where palsy shakes a few, sad, last gray hairs,
Where youth grows pale, and spectre-thin, and dies;
Where but to think is to be full of sorrow

And leaden-eyed despairs,
Where Beauty cannot keep her lustrous eyes,
Or new Love pine at them beyond to-morrow.

Away! away! for I will fly to thee,
Not charioted by Bacchus and his pards,
But on the viewless wings of Poesy,
Though the dull brain perplexes and retards:
Already with thee! tender is the night,
And haply the Queen-Moon is on her throne,
Cluster'd around by all her starry Fays;
But here there is no light,
Save what from heaven is with the breezes blown
Through verdurous glooms and winding mossy ways.

I cannot see what flowers are at my feet,
Nor what soft incense hangs upon the boughs,
But, in embalmèd darkness, guess each sweet
Wherewith the seasonable month endows
The grass, the thicket, and the fruit-tree wild;
White hawthorn, and the pastoral eglantine;
Fast fading violets cover'd up in leaves;
And mid-May's eldest child,
The coming musk-rose, full of dewy wine,
The murmurous haunt of flies on summer eves.

Darkling I listen; and, for many a time
I have been half in love with easeful Death,
Call'd him soft names in many a mused rhyme,
To take into the air my quiet breath;
Now more than ever seems it rich to die,
To cease upon the midnight with no pain,
While thou art pouring forth thy soul abroad
In such an ecstasy!
Still wouldst thou sing, and I have ears in vain—
To thy high requiem become a sod.

Thou wast not born for death, immortal Bird!
No hungry generations tread thee down;
The voice I hear this passing night was heard
In ancient days by emperor and clown:
Perhaps the self-same song that found a path
Through the sad heart of Ruth, when, sick for home,
She stood in tears amid the alien corn;
The same that oft-times hath
Charm'd magic casements, opening on the foam
Of perilous seas, in faery lands forlorn.

Forlorn! the very word is like a bell
To toll me back from thee to my sole self!
Adieu! the fancy cannot cheat so well
As she is fam'd to do, deceiving elf.
Adieu! adieu! thy plaintive anthem fades
Past the near meadows, over the still stream,
Up the hill-side; and now 'tis buried deep
In the next valley-glades:
Was it a vision, or a waking dream?
Fled is that music: —Do I wake or sleep?

To Autumn

Season of mists and mellow fruitfulness,
    Close bosom-friend of the maturing sun;
Conspiring with him how to load and bless
    With fruit the vines that round the thatch-eves run;
To bend with apples the moss'd cottage-trees,
    And fill all fruit with ripeness to the core;
        To swell the gourd, and plump the hazel shells
    With a sweet kernel; to set budding more,
And still more, later flowers for the bees,
Until they think warm days will never cease,
        For summer has o›er-brimm›d their clammy cells.

Who hath not seen thee oft amid thy store?
    Sometimes whoever seeks abroad may find
Thee sitting careless on a granary floor,
    Thy hair soft-lifted by the winnowing wind;
Or on a half-reap'd furrow sound asleep,
    Drows›d with the fume of poppies, while thy hook
        Spares the next swath and all its twined flowers:
And sometimes like a gleaner thou dost keep
    Steady thy laden head across a brook;
    Or by a cyder-press, with patient look,
        Thou watchest the last oozings hours by hours.

Where are the songs of spring? Ay, Where are they?
    Think not of them, thou hast thy music too, —
While barred clouds bloom the soft-dying day,
    And touch the stubble-plains with rosy hue;
Then in a wailful choir the small gnats mourn

Among the river sallows, borne aloft
Or sinking as the light wind lives or dies;
And full-grown lambs loud bleat from hilly bourn;
Hedge-crickets sing; and now with treble soft
The red-breast whistles from a garden-croft;
And gathering swallows twitter in the skies.

Elizabeth Barrett Browning (1806–61)

Born on March 6th, 1806, Elizabeth Barrett Browning was the oldest of twelve children at Coxhoe Hall in Durham, England. Her parents, Edward Moulton Barrett and Mary Graham Clarke, made their family fortune from Jamaican sugar plantations and the slave trade before Barrett Browning was born. Eventually, the family settled in Ledbury, Herefordshire, where their father built a mansion. Barrett Browning's family was deeply religious, and Christian themes play a prominent role in many of her poems.

At fourteen, Barrett Browning suffered multiple illnesses that she never recovered from, including a lung disease and a spinal injury that both led her to take morphine for the rest of her life and degraded her mobility. Despite these setbacks, Barrett Browning's first book was published in 1820—*The Battle of Marathon.* It included an epic poem inspired by Homer that she wrote after teaching herself Hebrew and learning about Greek culture.

Shortly after the publishing of Barrett Browning's *An Essay on Mind and Other Poems* in 1826 anonymously, her mother died. The death of her mother, along with the abolishment of slavery, caused the family to lose a lot of wealth, forcing them to sell their estate. In 1832 they moved to Sidmouth, Devon, but ultimately settled in London by 1838. During this time, Browning remained busy with the publishing of a translation of Aeschylus's *Prometheus Bound* (1833) and her famous *The Seraphim and Other Poems* (1838) that included her poem, "The Deserted Garden," which reflects on childlike wonder and what it is like to freely roam an abandoned garden.

In 1838, Barrett Browning's health problems forced her to move in with her brother, Edward, in Torquay, Devon. There she wrote a good amount, including "The Cry of the Children" in the 1840s, a poem that condemned child labor. Tragedy followed her again, however, when Edward drowned just two years after Barrett Browning had moved in with him. Her brother's death caused Barrett Browning to develop a fear of meeting anyone who was not a part of her intimate social group.

Within literary circles, Barrett Browning's name was well known and only increased in popularity once she released her second volume of poetry, *Poems, by Elizabeth Barrett Browning* (1844). This work caught the attention of Robert Browning, a Victorian poet known for his dramatic monologues. Browning got Barrett Browning's attention through a letter, opening with:

"I love your verses with all my heart, dear Miss Barrett, —and this is no off-hand complimentary letter that I shall write, —whatever else, no prompt matter-of-course recognition of your genius, and there a graceful and natural end of the thing."

—Robert Browning, January 10th, 1845.

After Robert Browning's first letter to Barrett Browning, the two continued to exchange over six hundred letters before their elopement in 1846. During that time, Barrett Browning was comfortable enough to meet Browning in early summer, just a few months after his first letter. The two kept their meetings and wedding a secret from Barrett Browning's father, but he never spoke with her again after finding out about her elopement with Robert Browning. Barrett Browning remained unforgiven up until her father's death in 1857.

After being cast off by Barrett Browning's father, the couple moved to Pisa, Italy. There, Barrett Browning wrote her poem protesting slavery in the United States: "The Runaway Slave at Pilgrim's Point" (1848) shortly before the birth of her only son, Robert Wiedemann Barrett Browning in 1849. The family travelled between Italy and London often during the last decade of Barrett Browning's life. She lived out her last years at her home, Casa Guidi, in Florence, Italy. She used her remaining years to focus on the political state of Italy, spiritualism, and the occult. She wrote "Casa Guidi Windows" (1851) from the point of view of the political events she witnessed from her home. The poem showed her enthusiasm for the freedom of Italian states, but disappointment in the liberalism that had been crushed in most of Italy. "A Curse for a Nation" (1860) offered another political critique, this time protesting U.S. slavery again.

Despite her strong feelings and her desire to constantly write, Barrett Browning still struggled from her childhood illnesses. After developing a severe cold, her degraded mobility and weak body could not heal itself. Eventually, Barrett Browning passed away in 1861. Robert Browning published her final works in *Last Poems* (1862) after her death, and her son collected the manuscripts of both his parents after his father's death in 1889. Today, Casa Guidi remains a historic landmark as the place where the Browning family produced their best poems.

Patience Taught by Nature

"O Dreary life!" we cry, "O dreary life!"
And still the generations of the birds
Sing through our sighing, and the flocks and herds
Serenely live while we are keeping strife
With Heaven's true purpose in us, as a knife
Against which we may struggle. Ocean girds
Unslackened the dry land: savannah-swards
Unweary sweep: hills watch, unworn; and rife
Meek leaves drop yearly from the forest-trees,
To show, above, the unwasted stars that pass
In their old glory. O thou God of old!
Grant me some smaller grace than comes to these; —
But so much patience, as a blade of grass
Grows by contented through the heat and cold.

The Deserted Garden

I mind me in the days departed,
How often underneath the sun
With childish bounds I used to run
    To a garden long deserted.

The beds and walks were vanish'd quite;
And wheresoe'er had struck the spade,
The greenest grasses Nature laid,
    To sanctify her right.

I call'd the place my wilderness,
For no one enter'd there but I.
The sheep look'd in, the grass to espy,
    And pass'd it ne'ertheless.

The trees were interwoven wild,
And spread their boughs enough about
To keep both sheep and shepherd out,
    But not a happy child.

Adventurous joy it was for me!
I crept beneath the boughs, and found
A circle smooth of mossy ground
    Beneath a poplar-tree.

Old garden rose-trees hedged it in,
Bedropt with roses waxen-white,
Well satisfied with dew and light,
    And careless to be seen.

Long years ago, it might befall,
When all the garden flowers were trim,
The grave old gardener prided him
    On these the most of all.

Some Lady, stately overmuch,
Here moving with a silken noise,
Has blush'd beside them at the voice
    That liken'd her to such.

Or these, to make a diadem,
She often may have pluck'd and twined;
Half-smiling as it came to mind,
    That few would look at them.

O, little thought that Lady proud,
A child would watch her fair white rose,
When buried lay her whiter brows,
    And silk was changed for shroud! —

Nor thought that gardener (full of scorns
For men unlearn'd and simple phrase)
A child would bring it all its praise,
    By creeping through the thorns!

To me upon my low moss seat,
Though never a dream the roses sent
Of science or love's compliment,
    I ween they smelt as sweet.

It did not move my grief to see
The trace of human step departed:
Because the garden was deserted,
    The blither place for me!

Friends, blame me not! a narrow ken
Hath childhood 'twixt the sun and sward:

We draw the moral afterward—
    We feel the gladness then.

And gladdest hours for me did glide
In silence at the rose-tree wall:
A thrush made gladness musical
    Upon the other side.

Nor he nor I did e'er incline
To peck or pluck the blossoms white: —
How should I know but that they might
    Lead lives as glad as mine?

To make my hermit-home complete,
I brought clear water from the spring
Praised in its own low murmuring,
    And cresses glossy wet.

And so, I thought, my likeness grew
(Without the melancholy tale)
To 'gentle hermit of the dale,'
    And Angelina too.

For oft I read within my nook
Such minstrel stories; till the breeze
Made sounds poetic in the trees,
    And then I shut the book.

If I shut this wherein I write,
I hear no more the wind athwart
Those trees, nor feel that childish heart
    Delighting in delight.

My childhood from my life is parted,
My footstep from the moss which drew
Its fairy circle round: anew
    The garden is deserted.

Another thrush may there rehearse
The madrigals which sweetest are;
No more for me! —myself afar
    Do sing a sadder verse.

Ah me! ah me! when erst I lay
In that child's-nest so greenly wrought,
I laugh'd unto myself and thought,
    'The time will pass away.'

And still I laugh'd, and did not fear
But that, whene'er was pass'd away
The childish time, some happier play
    My womanhood would cheer.

I knew the time would pass away;
And yet, beside the rose-tree wall,
Dear God, how seldom, if at all,
    Did I look up to pray!

The time is past: and now that grows
The cypress high among the trees,
And I behold white sepulchres
    As well as the white rose, —

When wiser, meeker thoughts are given,
And I have learnt to lift my face,
Reminded how earth's greenest place
    The colour draws from heaven, —

It something saith for earthly pain,
But more for heavenly promise free,
That I who was, would shrink to be
    That happy child again.

Ralph Waldo Emerson (1803–82)

Born on May 25th in 1803, Ralph Waldo Emerson was the leading proponent of American Transcendentalism. His father, William Emerson, was a clergyman, and his mother, Ruth Haskins, was strongly Anglican, making them prominent in Boston's religious scene. Because of his father's death in 1811 due to stomach cancer, Emerson was primarily raised by his mother and his aunt, Moody Emerson. His mother's Anglican faith, along with Anglican writers such as Robert Leighton and Samuel Taylor Coleridge, were just some of Emerson's influences.

In 1812, Emerson entered the Boston Public Latin School where his literary gifts were first recognized. In 1817, he enrolled in Harvard University and graduated four years later. During this time, he also did part-time study at the Harvard Divinity School. Emerson become a minister in 1826 and was fully ordained in 1829. Emerson's popularity as a preacher grew, but so did his questioning of Christian doctrines. That same year, Emerson married Ellen Tucker, but she died two years later from tuberculosis. Emerson became so distraught that his grief made him question his beliefs and profession even more. In 1832, Emerson had little interest in the Unitarianism, a branch of Christianity, and resigned from the ministry. He began searching for his own revelation and experience of God.

It was then that he journeyed to Europe to explore. In Paris, Antoine-Laurent de Jessieu's botany collection of natural species in developmental order deepened Emerson's belief that man and nature are connected spiritually. After visiting poets William Wordsworth and Samuel Taylor Coleridge, Emerson returned home in 1833 and began writing *Nature*. *Nature* focused on the individual's unique and intimate experience with nature and their connection to the "oversoul" that connects all living beings in the universe.

While working on *Nature*, Emerson continued his travels as a lecturer. In 1834, his lecture circuit took him to Plymouth, Massachusetts, where his met Lydia Jackson. The two were married in the Jackson family home only a year later.

After publishing *Nature* in 1836, Emerson became a major voice in American Transcendentalism and inspired other authors to find their own style of writing and become self-reliant in their decisions. Emerson was most productive in the 1840s. During this time, he started a family with Lydia along with composing some his most famous essays, "Self-Reliance," "Friendship," and "Experience." He also launched *The Dial*, a short-lived magazine that presented the latest ideas Transcendentalism had to offer.

Emerson spent his remaining life travelling to give lectures before his death in 1882. His voice inspired many. He advocated for the abolishment of slavery, and his works influenced Walt Whitman's poetry collection, *Leaves of Grass* (1855). Henry David Thoreau, who gained his love of nature and transcendental ideas from Emerson, produced his book, *Walden* (1854), after the reading Emerson's *Nature*.

Nature

By Ralph Waldo Emerson

Introduction

Our age is retrospective. It builds the sepulchres of the fathers. It writes biographies, histories, and criticism. The foregoing generations beheld God and nature face to face; we, through their eyes. Why should not we also enjoy an original relation to the universe? Why should not we have a poetry and philosophy of insight and not of tradition, and a religion by revelation to us, and not the history of theirs? Embosomed for a season in nature, whose floods of life stream around and through us, and invite us by the powers they supply, to action proportioned to nature, why should we grope among the dry bones of the past, or put the living generation into masquerade out of its faded wardrobe? The sun shines today also. There is more wool and flax in the fields. There are new lands, new men, new thoughts. Let us demand our own works and laws and worship.

Undoubtedly, we have no questions to ask which are unanswerable. We must trust the perfection of the creation so far, as to believe that whatever curiosity the order of things has awakened in our minds, the order of things can satisfy. Every man's condition is a solution in hieroglyphic to those inquiries he would put. He acts it as life, before he apprehends it as truth. In like manner, nature is already, in its forms and tendencies, describing its own design. Let us interrogate the great apparition, that shines so peacefully around us. Let us inquire, to what end is nature?

All science has one aim, namely, to find a theory of nature. We have theories of races and of functions, but scarcely yet a remote approach to an idea of creation. We are now so far from the road to truth, that religious teachers dispute and hate each other, and speculative men are esteemed unsound and frivolous. But to a sound judgment, the most abstract truth is the most practical. Whenever a true theory appears, it will be its own evidence. Its test is, that it will explain all phenomena.

Now many are thought not only unexplained but inexplicable; as language, sleep, madness, dreams, beasts, sex.

Philosophically considered, the universe is composed of Nature and the Soul. Strictly speaking, therefore, all that is separate from us, all which Philosophy distinguishes as the NOT ME, that is, both nature and art, all other men and my own body, must be ranked under this name, NATURE. In enumerating the values of nature and casting up their sum, I shall use the word in both senses; —in its common and in its philosophical import. In inquiries so general as our present one, the inaccuracy is not material; no confusion of thought will occur. *Nature*, in the common sense, refers to essences unchanged by man; space, the air, the river, the leaf. *Art* is applied to the mixture of his will with the same things, as in a house, a canal, a statue, a picture. But his operations taken together are so insignificant, a little chipping, baking, patching, and washing, that in an impression so grand as that of the world on the human mind, they do not vary the result.

Chapter I: Nature

To go into solitude, a man needs to retire as much from his chamber as from society. I am not solitary whilst I read and write, though nobody is with me. But if a man would be alone, let him look at the stars. The rays that come from those heavenly worlds, will separate between him and what he touches. One might think the atmosphere was made transparent with this design, to give man, in the heavenly bodies, the perpetual presence of the sublime. Seen in the streets of cities, how great they are! If the stars should appear one night in a thousand years, how would men believe and adore; and preserve for many generations the remembrance of the city of God which had been shown! But every night come out these envoys of beauty, and light the universe with their admonishing smile.

The stars awaken a certain reverence, because though always present, they are inaccessible; but all natural objects make a kindred impression, when the mind is open to their influence. Nature never wears a mean appearance. Neither does the wisest man extort her secret, and lose his curiosity by finding out all her perfection. Nature never became a toy to a wise spirit. The flowers, the animals, the mountains, reflected the wisdom of his best hour, as much as they had delighted the simplicity of his childhood.

When we speak of nature in this manner, we have a distinct but most poetical sense in the mind. We mean the integrity of impression made by manifold natural objects. It is this which distinguishes the stick of timber of the woodcutter, from the tree of the poet. The charming landscape which I saw this morning, is indubitably made up of some twenty or thirty farms. Miller owns this field, Locke that, and Manning the woodland beyond. But none of them owns the landscape. There is a property in the horizon which no man has but he whose eye can integrate all the parts, that is, the poet. This is the best part of these men's farms, yet to this their warranty-deeds give no title.

To speak truly, few adult persons can see nature. Most persons do not see the sun. At least they have a very superficial seeing. The sun illuminates only the eye of the man, but shines into the eye and the heart of the child. The lover of nature is he whose inward and outward senses are still truly adjusted to each other; who has retained the spirit of infancy even into the era of manhood. His intercourse with heaven and earth becomes part of his daily food. In the presence of nature, a wild delight runs through the man, in spite of real sorrows. Nature says, —he is my creature, and maugre all his impertinent griefs, he shall be glad with me. Not the sun or the summer alone, but every hour and season yields its tribute of delight; for every hour and change corresponds to and authorizes a different state of the mind, from breathless noon to grimmest midnight. Nature is a setting that fits equally well a comic or a mourning piece. In good health, the air is a cordial of incredible virtue. Crossing a bare common, in snow puddles, at twilight, under a clouded sky, without having in my thoughts any occurrence of special good fortune, I have enjoyed a perfect exhilaration. I am glad to the brink of fear. In the woods too, a man casts off his years, as the snake his slough, and at what period soever of life, is always a child. In the woods, is perpetual youth. Within these plantations of God, a decorum and sanctity reign, a perennial festival is dressed, and the guest sees not how he should tire of them in a thousand years. In the woods, we return to reason and faith. There I feel that nothing can befall me in life, no disgrace, no calamity, (leaving me my eyes), which nature cannot repair. Standing on the bare ground, my head bathed by the blithe air, and uplifted into infinite space, all mean egotism vanishes. I become a transparent eyeball; I am nothing; I see all; the currents of the Universal Being circulate through me; I am part or particle of God. The name of the

nearest friend sounds then foreign and accidental: to be brothers, to be acquaintances, master or servant, is then a trifle and a disturbance. I am the lover of uncontained and immortal beauty. In the wilderness, I find something more dear and connate than in streets or villages. In the tranquil landscape, and especially in the distant line of the horizon, man beholds somewhat as beautiful as his own nature.

The greatest delight which the fields and woods minister, is the suggestion of an occult relation between man and the vegetable. I am not alone and unacknowledged. They nod to me, and I to them. The waving of the boughs in the storm, is new to me and old. It takes me by surprise and yet is not unknown. Its effect is like that of a higher thought or a better emotion coming over me, when I deemed, I was thinking justly or doing right.

Yet it is certain that the power to produce this delight, does not reside in nature, but in man, or in a harmony of both. It is necessary to use these pleasures with great temperance. For, nature is not always tricked in holiday attire, but the same scene which yesterday breathed perfume and glittered as for the frolic of the nymphs, is overspread with melancholy today. Nature always wears the colors of the spirit. To a man laboring under calamity, the heat of his own fire hath sadness in it. Then, there is a kind of contempt of the landscape felt by him who has just lost by death a dear friend. The sky is less grand as it shuts down over less worth in the population.

Chapter II: Commodity

Whoever considers the final cause of the world will discern a multitude of uses that result. They all admit of being thrown into one of the following classes: Commodity; Beauty; Language; and Discipline.

Under the general name of Commodity, I rank all those advantages which our senses owe to nature. This, of course, is a benefit which is temporary and mediate, not ultimate, like its service to the soul. Yet although low, it is perfect in its kind, and is the only use of nature which all men apprehend. The misery of man appears like childish petulance, when we explore the steady and prodigal provision that has been made for his support and delight on this green ball which floats him through the heavens. What angels invented these splendid ornaments, these rich conveniences, this ocean of air above, this ocean of water beneath, this firmament of earth between? This zodiac of lights, this tent of dropping clouds, this striped coat of climates, this fourfold year? Beasts, fire, water, stones, and corn serve him. The field is at once his floor, his work-yard, his play-ground, his garden, and his bed.

"More servants wait on man
Than he'll take notice of."

Nature, in its ministry to man, is not only the material, but is also the process and the result. All the parts incessantly work into each other's hands for the profit of man. The wind sows the seed; the sun evaporates the sea; the wind blows the vapor to the field; the ice, on the other side of the planet, condenses rain on this; the rain feeds the plant; the plant feeds the animal; and thus, the endless circulations of the divine charity nourish man.

The useful arts are reproductions or new combinations by the wit of man, of the same natural benefactors. He no longer waits for favoring gales, but by means of steam, he realizes the fable of Aeolus's bag, and carries the two and thirty winds in the boiler of his boat. To diminish friction, he paves the road with iron bars, and, mounting a coach with a shipload of men, animals, and merchandise behind him, he darts through the country, from town to town, like an eagle or a swallow through the air. By the aggregate of these aids, how is the face of the world changed, from the era of Noah to that of Napoleon! The private poor man hath cities, ships, canals, bridges, built for him. He goes to the post office, and the human race run on his errands; to the bookshop, and the human race read and write of all that happens, for him; to the courthouse, and nations repair his wrongs. He sets his house upon the road, and the human race go forth every morning, and shovel out the snow, and cut a path for him.

But there is no need of specifying particulars in this class of uses. The catalogue is endless, and the examples so obvious, that I shall leave them to the reader's reflection, with the general remark, that this mercenary benefit is one which has respect to a farther good. A man is fed, not that he may be fed, but that he may work.

Chapter III: Beauty

A NOBLER WANT OF MAN IS SERVED BY NATURE, namely, the love of Beauty.

The ancient Greeks called the world *κοσμος*, beauty. Such is the constitution of all things, or such the plastic power of the human eye, that the primary forms, as the sky, the mountain, the tree, the animal, give us a delight in and for themselves; a pleasure arising from outline, color, motion, and grouping. This seems partly owing to the eye itself. The eye is the best of artists. By the mutual action of its structure and of the laws of light, perspective is produced, which integrates every mass of objects, of what character soever, into a well colored and shaded globe, so that where the particular objects are mean and unaffecting, the landscape which they compose, is round and symmetrical. And as the eye is the best composer, so light is the first of painters. There is no object so foul that intense light will not make beautiful. And the stimulus it affords to the sense, and a sort of infinitude which it hath, like space and time, make all matter gay. Even the corpse has its own beauty. But besides this general grace diffused over nature, almost all the individual forms are agreeable to the eye, as is proved by our endless imitations of some of them, as the acorn, the grape, the pine-cone, the wheat-ear, the egg, the wings and forms of most birds, the lion's claw, the serpent, the butterfly, sea-shells, flames, clouds, buds, leaves, and the forms of many trees, as the palm.

For better consideration, we may distribute the aspects of Beauty in a threefold manner.

1. First, the simple perception of natural forms is a delight. The influence of the forms and actions in nature, is so needful to man, that, in its lowest functions, it seems to lie on the confines of commodity

and beauty. To the body and mind which have been cramped by noxious work or company, nature is medicinal and restores their tone. The tradesman, the attorney comes out of the din and craft of the street, and sees the sky and the woods, and is a man again. In their eternal calm, he finds himself. The health of the eye seems to demand a horizon. We are never tired, so long as we can see far enough.

But in other hours, Nature satisfies by its loveliness, and without any mixture of corporeal benefit. I see the spectacle of morning from the hill-top over against my house, from daybreak to sunrise, with emotions which an angel might share. The long slender bars of cloud float like fishes in the sea of crimson light. From the earth, as a shore, I look out into that silent sea. I seem to partake its rapid transformations: the active enchantment reaches my dust, and I dilate and conspire with the morning wind. How does Nature deify us with a few and cheap elements! Give me health and a day, and I will make the pomp of emperors ridiculous. The dawn is my Assyria; the sunset and moonrise my Paphos, and unimaginable realms of faerie; broad noon shall be my England of the senses and the understanding; the night shall be my Germany of mystic philosophy and dreams.

Not less excellent, except for our less susceptibility in the afternoon, was the charm, last evening, of a January sunset. The western clouds divided and subdivided themselves into pink flakes modulated with tints of unspeakable softness; and the air had so much life and sweetness, that it was a pain to come within doors. What was it that nature would say? Was there no meaning in the live repose of the valley behind the mill, and which Homer or Shakespeare could not reform for me in words? The leafless trees become spires of flame in the sunset, with the blue east for their background, and the stars of the dead calices of flowers, and every withered stem and stubble rimed with frost, contribute something to the mute music.

The inhabitants of cities suppose that the country landscape is pleasant only half the year. I please myself with the graces of the winter scenery, and believe that we are as much touched by it as by the genial influences of summer. To the attentive eye, each moment of the year has its own beauty, and in the same field, it beholds, every hour, a picture which was never seen before, and which shall never be seen again. The heavens change every moment, and reflect their glory or gloom on the plains beneath. The state of the crop in the surrounding farms alters the expression of the earth from week to week. The succession of native plants in the pastures and roadsides, which makes the silent clock by which time tells the summer hours, will make even the divisions of the day sensible to a keen observer. The tribes of birds and insects, like the plants punctual to their time, follow each other, and the year has room for all. By water-courses, the variety is greater. In July, the blue Pontederia or pickerel-weed blooms in large beds in the shallow parts of our pleasant river, and swarms with yellow butterflies in continual motion. Art cannot rival this pomp of purple and gold. Indeed, the river is a perpetual gala, and boasts each month a new ornament.

But this beauty of Nature, which is seen and felt as beauty, is the least part. The shows of day, the dewy morning, the rainbow, mountains, orchards in blossom, stars, moonlight, shadows in still water, and the like, if too eagerly hunted, become shows merely, and mock us with their unreality. Go out of the house to see the moon, and 't is mere tinsel; it will not please as when its light shines upon your necessary journey. The beauty that shimmers in the yellow afternoons of October, whoever could clutch it? Go forth to find it, and it is gone: it is only a mirage as you look from the windows of diligence.

2. The presence of a higher, namely, of the spiritual element is essential to its perfection. The high and divine beauty which can be loved without effeminacy, is that which is found in combination with the human will. Beauty is the mark God sets upon virtue. Every natural action is graceful. Every heroic act is also decent, and causes the place and the bystanders to shine. We are taught by great actions that the universe is the property of every individual in it. Every rational creature has all nature for his dowry and estate. It is his, if he will. He may divest himself of it; he may creep into a corner, and abdicate his kingdom, as most men do, but he is entitled to the world by his constitution. In proportion to the energy of his thought and will, he takes up the world into himself. "All those things for which men plough, build, or sail, obey virtue;" said Sallust. "The winds and waves," said Gibbon, "are always on the side of the ablest navigators." So are the sun and moon and all the stars of heaven. When a noble act is done,—per-

chance in a scene of great natural beauty; when Leonidas and his three hundred martyrs consume one day in dying, and the sun and moon come each and look at them once in the steep defile of Thermopylae; when Arnold Winkelried, in the high Alps, under the shadow of the avalanche, gathers in his side a sheaf of Austrian spears to break the line for his comrades; are not these heroes entitled to add the beauty of the scene to the beauty of the deed? When the bark of Columbus nears the shore of America; —before it, the beach lined with savages, fleeing out of all their huts of cane; the sea behind; and the purple mountains of the Indian Archipelago around, can we separate the man from the living picture? Does not the New World clothe his form with her palm-groves and savannahs as fit drapery? Ever does natural beauty steal in like air, and envelope great actions. When Sir Harry Vane was dragged up the Tower-hill, sitting on a sled, to suffer death, as the champion of the English laws, one of the multitude cried out to him, "You never sate on so glorious a seat." Charles II., to intimidate the citizens of London, caused the patriot Lord Russel to be drawn in an open coach, through the principal streets of the city, on his way to the scaffold. "But," his biographer says, "the multitude imagined they saw liberty and virtue sitting by his side." In private places, among sordid objects, an act of truth or heroism seems at once to draw to itself the sky as its temple, the sun as its candle. Nature stretcheth out her arms to embrace man, only let his thoughts be of equal greatness. Willingly does she follow his steps with the rose and the violet, and bend her lines of grandeur and grace to the decoration of her darling child. Only let his thoughts be of equal scope, and the frame will suit the picture. A virtuous man is in unison with her works, and makes the central figure of the visible sphere. Homer, Pindar, Socrates, Phocion, associate themselves fitly in our memory with the geography and climate of Greece. The visible heavens and earth sympathize with Jesus. And in common life, whosoever has seen a person of powerful character and happy genius, will have remarked how easily he took all things along with him, —the persons, the opinions, and the day, and nature became ancillary to a man.

3. There is still another aspect under which the beauty of the world may be viewed, namely, as it becomes an object of the intellect.

Beside the relation of things to virtue, they have a relation to thought. The intellect searches out the absolute order of things as they stand in the mind of God, and without the colors of affection. The intellectual and the active powers seem to succeed each other, and the exclusive activity of the one, generates the exclusive activity of the other. There is something unfriendly in each to the other, but they are like the alternate periods of feeding and working in animals; each prepares and will be followed by the other. Therefore does beauty, which, in relation to actions, as we have seen, comes unsought, and comes because it is unsought, remain for the apprehension and pursuit of the intellect; and then again, in its turn, of the active power. Nothing divine dies. All good is eternally reproductive. The beauty of nature reforms itself in the mind, and not for barren contemplation, but for new creation.

All men are in some degree impressed by the face of the world; some men even to delight. This love of beauty is Taste. Others have the same love in such excess, that, not content with admiring, they seek to embody it in new forms. The creation of beauty is Art.

The production of a work of art throws a light upon the mystery of humanity. A work of art is an abstract or epitome of the world. It is the result or expression of nature, in miniature. For, although the works of nature are innumerable and all different, the result or the expression of them all is similar and single. Nature is a sea of forms radically alike and even unique. A leaf, a sunbeam, a landscape, the ocean, make an analogous impression on the mind. What is common to them all, that perfectness and harmony, is beauty. The standard of beauty is the entire circuit of natural forms, —the totality of nature; which the Italians expressed by defining beauty "il piu nell' uno." Nothing is quite beautiful alone: nothing but is beautiful in the whole. A single object is only so far beautiful as it suggests this universal grace. The poet, the painter, the sculptor, the musician, the architect, seek each to concentrate this radiance of the world on one point, and each in his several work to satisfy the love of beauty which stimulates him to produce. Thus is Art, a nature passed through the alembic of man. Thus, in art, does nature work through the will of a man filled with the beauty of her first works.

The world thus exists to the soul to satisfy the desire of beauty. This element I call an ultimate end. No reason can be asked or given why the soul seeks beauty. Beauty, in its largest and profoundest sense, is one expression for the universe. God is the all-fair. Truth, and goodness, and beauty, are but different faces of the same All. But beauty in nature is not ultimate. It is the herald of inward and eternal beauty, and is not alone a solid and satisfactory good. It must stand as a part, and not as yet the last or highest expression of the final cause of Nature.

Chapter IV: Language

Language is a third use which Nature subserves to man. Nature is the vehicle, and threefold degree.

1. Words are signs of natural facts.
2. Particular natural facts are symbols of particular spiritual facts.
3. Nature is the symbol of spirit.

1. Words are signs of natural facts. The use of natural history is to give us aid in supernatural history: the use of the outer creation, to give us language for the beings and changes of the inward creation. Every word which is used to express a moral or intellectual fact, if traced to its root, is found to be borrowed from some material appearance. *Right* means *straight*; *wrong* means *twisted*. Spirit primarily means *wind*; *transgression*, the crossing of a *line*; *supercilious*, the *raising of the eyebrow*. We say the heart to express emotion, the head to denote thought; and thought and emotion are words borrowed from sensible things, and now appropriated to spiritual nature. Most of the process by which this transformation is made, is hidden from us in the remote time when language was framed; but the same tendency may be daily observed in children. Children and savages use only nouns or names of things, which they convert into verbs, and apply to analogous mental acts.

2. But this origin of all words that convey a spiritual import, so conspicuous a fact in the history of language, is our least debt to nature. It is not words only that are emblematic; it is things which are emblematic. Every natural fact is a symbol of some spiritual fact. Every appearance in nature corresponds to some state of the mind, and

that state of the mind can only be described by presenting that natural appearance as its picture. An enraged man is a lion, a cunning man is a fox, a firm man is a rock, a learned man is a torch. A lamb is innocence; a snake is subtle spite; flowers express to us the delicate affections. Light and darkness are our familiar expression for knowledge and ignorance, and heat for love. Visible distance behind and before us, is respectively our image of memory and hope.

Who looks upon a river in a meditative hour, and is not reminded of the flux of all things? Throw a stone into the stream, and the circles that propagate themselves are the beautiful type of all influence. Man is conscious of a universal soul within or behind his individual life, wherein, as in a firmament, the natures of Justice, Truth, Love, Freedom, arise and shine. This universal soul, he calls Reason: it is not mine, or thine, or his, but we are its; we are its property and men. And the blue sky in which the private earth is buried, the sky with its eternal calm, and full of everlasting orbs, is the type of Reason. That which, intellectually considered, we call Reason, considered in relation to nature, we call Spirit. Spirit is the Creator. Spirit hath life in itself. And man in all ages and countries, embodies it in his language, as the FATHER.

It is easily seen that there is nothing lucky or capricious in these analogies, but that they are constant, and pervade nature. These are not the dreams of a few poets, here and there, but man is an analogist, and studies relations in all objects. He is placed in the centre of beings, and a ray of relation passes from every other being to him. And neither can man be understood without these objects, nor these objects without man. All the facts in natural history taken by themselves, have no value, but are barren, like a single sex. But marry it to human history, and it is full of life. Whole Floras, all Linnaeus' and Buffon's volumes, are dry catalogues of facts; but the most trivial of these facts, the habit of a plant, the organs, or work, or noise of an insect, applied to the illustration of a fact in intellectual philosophy, or, in any way associated to human nature, affects us in the most lively and agreeable manner. The seed of a plant, —to what affecting analogies in the nature of man, is that little fruit made use of, in all discourse, up to the voice of Paul, who calls the human corpse a seed, —"It is sown a natural body; it is raised a spiritual body." The motion of the earth round its axis, and round the sun, makes the day, and the year. These are certain amounts of brute light and heat. But is there no intent of an analogy between man's life and the seasons? And do the seasons gain no grandeur or pathos from that analogy? The instincts of the ant are very unimportant, considered as the ant's; but the moment a ray of relation is seen to extend from it to man, and the little drudge is seen to be a monitor, a little body with a mighty heart, then all its habits, even that said to be recently observed, that it never sleeps, become sublime.

Because of this radical correspondence between visible things and human thoughts, savages, who have only what is necessary, converse in figures. As we go back in history, language becomes more picturesque, until its infancy, when it is all poetry; or all spiritual facts are represented by natural symbols. The same symbols are found to make the original elements of all languages. It has moreover been observed, that the idioms of all languages approach each other in passages of the greatest eloquence and power. And as this is the first language, so is it the last. This immediate dependence of language upon nature, this conversion of an outward phenomenon into a type of somewhat in human life, never loses its power to affect us. It is this which gives that piquancy to the conversation of a strong-natured farmer or back-woodsman, which all men relish.

A man's power to connect his thought with its proper symbol, and so to utter it, depends on the simplicity of his character, that is, upon his love of truth, and his desire to communicate it without loss. The corruption of man is followed by the corruption of language. When simplicity of character and the sovereignty of ideas is broken up by the prevalence of secondary desires, the desire of riches, of pleasure, of power, and of praise,—and duplicity and falsehood take place of simplicity and truth, the power over nature as an interpreter of the will, is in a degree lost; new imagery ceases to be created, and old words are perverted to stand for things which are not; a paper currency is employed, when there is no bullion in the vaults. In due time, the fraud is manifest, and words lose all power to stimulate the understanding or the affections. Hundreds of writers may be found in every long-civilized nation, who for a short time believe, and make others believe, that they see and utter truths, who do not of themselves clothe one thought in its natural garment, but who feed unconsciously on the language created by the primary writers of the country, those, namely, who hold primarily on nature.

But wise men pierce this rotten diction and fasten words again to visible things; so that picturesque language is at once a commanding certificate that he who employs it, is a man in alliance with truth and God. The moment our discourse rises above the ground line of familiar facts, and is inflamed with passion or exalted by thought, it clothes itself in images. A man conversing in earnest, if he watch his intellectual processes, will find that a material image, more or less luminous, arises in his mind, cotemporaneous with every thought, which furnishes the vestment of the thought. Hence, good writing and brilliant discourse are perpetual allegories. This imagery is spontaneous. It is the blending of experience with the present action of the mind. It is proper creation. It is the working of the Original Cause through the instruments he has already made.

These facts may suggest the advantage which the country life possesses for a powerful mind over the artificial and curtailed life of cities. We know more from nature than we can at will communicate. Its light flows into the mind evermore, and we forget its presence. The poet, the orator, bred in the woods, whose senses have been nourished by their fair and appeasing changes, year after year, without design and without heed, shall not lose their lesson altogether, in the roar of cities or the broil of politics. Long hereafter, amidst agitation and terror in national councils, in the hour of revolution, —these solemn images shall reappear in their morning lustre, as fit symbols and words of the thoughts which the passing events shall awaken. At the call of a noble sentiment, again the woods wave, the pines murmur, the river rolls and shines, and the cattle low upon the mountains, as he saw and heard them in his infancy. And with these forms, the spells of persuasion, the keys of power are put into his hands.

3. We are thus assisted by natural objects in the expression of particular meanings. But how great a language to convey such pepper-corn informations! Did it need such noble races of creatures, this profusion of forms, this host of orbs in heaven, to furnish man with the dictionary and grammar of his municipal speech? Whilst we use this grand cipher to expedite the affairs of our pot and kettle, we feel

that we have not yet put it to its use, neither are able. We are like travellers using the cinders of a volcano to roast their eggs. Whilst we see that it always stands ready to clothe what we would say, we cannot avoid the question, whether the characters are not significant of themselves. Have mountains, and waves, and skies, no significance but what we consciously give them, when we employ them as emblems of our thoughts? The world is emblematic. Parts of speech are metaphors, because the whole of nature is a metaphor of the human mind. The laws of moral nature answer to those of matter as face to face in a glass. "The visible world and the relation of its parts, is the dial plate of the invisible." The axioms of physics translate the laws of ethics. Thus, "the whole is greater than its part;" "reaction is equal to action;" "the smallest weight may be made to lift the greatest, the difference of weight being compensated by time;" and many the like propositions, which have an ethical as well as physical sense. These propositions have a much more extensive and universal sense when applied to human life, than when confined to technical use.

In like manner, the memorable words of history, and the proverbs of nations, consist usually of a natural fact, selected as a picture or parable of a moral truth. Thus; A rolling stone gathers no moss; A bird in the hand is worth two in the bush; A cripple in the right way, will beat a racer in the wrong; Make hay while the sun shines; 'T is hard to carry a full cup even; Vinegar is the son of wine; The last ounce broke the camel's back; Long-lived trees make roots first;—and the like. In their primary sense these are trivial facts, but we repeat them for the value of their analogical import. What is true of proverbs, is true of all fables, parables, and allegories.

This relation between the mind and matter is not fancied by some poet, but stands in the will of God, and so is free to be known by all men. It appears to men, or it does not appear. When in fortunate hours we ponder this miracle, the wise man doubts, if, at all other times, he is not blind and deaf;

"Can these things be,
And overcome us like a summer's cloud,
Without our special wonder?"

For the universe becomes transparent, and the light of higher laws than its own, shines through it. It is the standing problem which has exercised the wonder and the study of every fine genius since the world began; from the era of the Egyptians and the Brahmins, to that of Pythagoras, of Plato, of Bacon, of Leibnitz, of Swedenborg. There sits the Sphinx at the roadside, and from age to age, as each prophet comes by, he tries his fortune at reading her riddle. There seems to be a necessity in spirit to manifest itself in material forms; and day and night, river and storm, beast and bird, acid and alkali, preexist in necessary Ideas in the mind of God, and are what they are by virtue of preceding affections, in the world of spirit. A Fact is the end or last issue of spirit. The visible creation is the terminus or the circumference of the invisible world. "Material objects," said a French philosopher, "are necessarily kinds of scoriae of the substantial thoughts of the Creator, which must always preserve an exact relation to their first origin; in other words, visible nature must have a spiritual and moral side.»

This doctrine is abstruse, and though the images of "garment," "scoriae," "mirror," &c., may stimulate the fancy, we must summon the aid of subtler and more vital expositors to make it plain. "Every scripture is to be interpreted by the same spirit which gave it forth," is the fundamental law of criticism. A life in harmony with nature, the love of truth and of virtue, will purge the eyes to understand her text. By degrees we may come to know the primitive sense of the permanent objects of nature, so that the world shall be to us an open book, and every form significant of its hidden life and final cause.

A new interest surprises us, whilst, under the view now suggested, we contemplate the fearful extent and multitude of objects; since "every object rightly seen, unlocks a new faculty of the soul." That, which was unconscious truth, becomes, when interpreted and defined in an object, a part of the domain of knowledge, a new weapon in the magazine of power.

Chapter V: Discipline

In view of the significance of nature, we arrive at once at a new fact, that nature is a discipline. This use of the world includes the preceding uses, as parts of itself.

Space, time, society, labor, climate, food, locomotion, the animals, the mechanical forces, give us sincerest lessons, day by day, whose meaning is unlimited. They educate both the Understanding and the Reason. Every property of matter is a school for understanding, its solidity or resistance, its inertia, its extension, its figure, its divisibility. The understanding adds, divides, combines, measures, and finds nutriment and room for its activity in this worthy scene. Meantime, Reason transfers all these lessons into its own world of thought, by perceiving the analogy that marries Matter and Mind.

1. Nature is a discipline of the understanding in intellectual truths. Our dealing with sensible objects is a constant exercise in the necessary lessons of difference, of likeness, of order, of being and seeming, of progressive arrangement; of ascent from particular to general; of combination to one end of manifold forces. Proportioned to the importance of the organ to be formed, is the extreme care with which its tuition is provided, a care pretermitted in no single case. What tedious training, day after day, year after year, never ending, to form the common sense; what continual reproduction of annoyances, inconveniences, dilemmas; what rejoicing over us of little men; what disputing of prices, what reckonings of interest,—and all to form the Hand of the mind;—to instruct us that "good thoughts are no better than good dreams, unless they be executed!"

The same good office is performed by Property and its filial systems of debt and credit. Debt, grinding debt, whose iron face the widow, the orphan, and the sons of genius fear and hate; debt, which consumes so much time, which so cripples and disheartens a great spirit with cares that seem so base, is a preceptor whose lessons cannot be forgone, and is needed most by those who suffer from it most. Moreover, property, which has been well compared to snow, "if it fall level today, it will be blown into drifts to-morrow," is the surface action of internal machinery, like the index on the face of a clock. Whilst now it is the gymnastics of the understanding, it is hiving in the foresight of the spirit, experience in profounder laws.

The whole character and fortune of the individual are affected by the least inequalities in the culture of the understanding; for example, in the perception of differences. Therefore, is Space, and therefore Time, that man may know that things are not huddled and lumped, but sundered and individual. A bell and a plough have each their use, and neither can do the office of the other. Water is good to drink, coal to burn, wool to wear; but wool cannot be drunk, nor water spun, nor coal eaten. The wise man shows his wisdom in separation, in gradation, and his scale of creatures and of merits is as wide as nature. The foolish have no range in their scale, but suppose every man is as every other man. What is not good they call the worst, and what is not hateful, they call the best.

In like manner, what good heed, nature forms in us! She pardons no mistakes. Her yea is yea, and her nay, nay.

The first steps in Agriculture, Astronomy, Zoölogy, (those first steps which the farmer, the hunter, and the sailor take,) teach that nature's dice are always loaded; that in her heaps and rubbish are concealed sure and useful results.

How calmly and genially the mind apprehends one after another the laws of physics! What noble emotions dilate the mortal as he enters into the counsels of the creation, and feels by knowledge the privilege to BE! His insight refines him. The beauty of nature shines in his own breast. Man is greater that he can see this, and the universe less, because Time and Space relations vanish as laws are known.

Here again we are impressed and even daunted by the immense Universe to be explored. "What we know, is a point to what we do not know." Open any recent journal of science, and weigh the problems suggested concerning Light, Heat, Electricity, Magnetism, Physiology,

Geology, and judge whether the interest of natural science is likely to be soon exhausted.

Passing by many particulars of the discipline of nature, we must not omit to specify two.

The exercise of the Will or the lesson of power is taught in every event. From the child's successive possession of his several senses up to the hour when he saith, "Thy will be done!" he is learning the secret, that he can reduce under his will, not only particular events, but great classes, nay the whole series of events, and so conform all facts to his character. Nature is thoroughly mediate. It is made to serve. It receives the dominion of man as meekly as the ass on which the Saviour rode. It offers all its kingdoms to man as the raw material which he may mould into what is useful. Man is never weary of working it up. He forges the subtile and delicate air into wise and melodious words and gives them wing as angels of persuasion and command. One after another, his victorious thought comes up with and reduces all things, until the world becomes, at last, only a realized will, —the double of the man.

2. Sensible objects conform to the premonitions of Reason and reflect the conscience. All things are moral; and in their boundless changes have an unceasing reference to spiritual nature. Therefore is nature glorious with form, color, and motion, that every globe in the remotest heaven; every chemical change from the rudest crystal up to the laws of life; every change of vegetation from the first principle of growth in the eye of a leaf, to the tropical forest and antediluvian coal-mine; every animal function from the sponge up to Hercules, shall hint or thunder to man the laws of right and wrong, and echo the Ten Commandments. Therefore, is nature ever the ally of Religion: lends all her pomp and riches to the religious sentiment. Prophet and priest, David, Isaiah, Jesus, have drawn deeply from this source. This ethical character so penetrates the bone and marrow of nature, as to seem the end for which it was made. Whatever private purpose is answered by any member or part, this is its public and universal function, and is never omitted. Nothing in nature is exhausted in its first use. When a thing has served an end to the uttermost, it is wholly new for an ulterior service. In God, every end is converted into a new means. Thus the

use of commodity, regarded by itself, is mean and squalid. But it is to the mind an education in the doctrine of Use, namely, that a thing is good only so far as it serves; that a conspiring of parts and efforts to the production of an end is essential to any being. The first and gross manifestation of this truth, is our inevitable and hated training in values and wants, in corn and meat.

It has already been illustrated that every natural process is a version of a moral sentence. The moral law lies at the centre of nature and radiates to the circumference. It is the pith and marrow of every substance, every relation, and every process. All things with which we deal, preach to us. What is a farm but a mute gospel? The chaff and the wheat, weeds and plants, blight, rain, insects, sun, it is a sacred emblem from the first furrow of spring to the last stack which the snow of winter overtakes in the fields. But the sailor, the shepherd, the miner, the merchant, in their several resorts, have each an experience precisely parallel, and leading to the same conclusion: because all organizations are radically alike. Nor can it be doubted that this moral sentiment which thus scents the air, grows in the grain, and impregnates the waters of the world, is caught by man and sinks into his soul. The moral influence of nature upon every individual is that amount of truth which it illustrates to him. Who can estimate this? Who can guess how much firmness the sea-beaten rock has taught the fisherman? how much tranquility has been reflected to man from the azure sky, over whose unspotted deeps the winds forevermore drive flocks of stormy clouds, and leave no wrinkle or stain? how much industry and providence and affection we have caught from the pantomime of brutes? What a searching preacher of self-command is the varying phenomenon of Health!

Herein is especially apprehended the unity of Nature, the unity in variety, which meets us everywhere. All the endless variety of things make an identical impression. Xenophanes complained in his old age, that, look where he would, all things hastened back to Unity. He was weary of seeing the same entity in the tedious variety of forms. The fable of Proteus has a cordial truth. A leaf, a drop, a crystal, a moment of time is related to the whole, and partakes of the perfection of the whole. Each particle is a microcosm and faithfully renders the likeness of the world.

Not only resemblances exist in things whose analogy is obvious, as when we detect the type of the human hand in the flipper of the fossil saurus, but also in objects wherein there is great superficial unlikeness. Thus, architecture is called "frozen music," by De Stael and Goethe. Vitruvius thought an architect should be a musician. "A Gothic church," said Coleridge, "is a petrified religion." Michael Angelo maintained that, to an architect, a knowledge of anatomy is essential. In Haydn's oratorios, the notes present to the imagination not only motions, as, of the snake, the stag, and the elephant, but colors also, as the green grass. The law of harmonic sounds reappears in the harmonic colors. The granite is differenced in its laws only by the more or less of heat, from the river that wears it away. The river, as it flows, resembles the air that flows over it; the air resembles the light which traverses it with more subtile currents; the light resembles the heat which rides with it through Space. Each creature is only a modification of the other; the likeness in them is more than the difference, and their radical law is one and the same. A rule of one art, or a law of one organization, holds true throughout nature. So intimate is this Unity that, it is easily seen, lies under the undermost garment of nature and betrays its source in Universal Spirit. For, it pervades Thought also. Every universal truth which we express in words implies or supposes every other truth. *Omne verum vero consonat.* It is like a great circle on a sphere, comprising all possible circles, which, however, may be drawn, and comprise it, in like manner. Every such truth is the absolute Ens seen from one side. But it has innumerable sides.

The central Unity is still more conspicuous in actions. Words are finite organs of the infinite mind. They cannot cover the dimensions of what is in truth. They break, chop, and impoverish it. An action is the perfection and publication of thought. A right action seems to fill the eye, and to be related to all nature. "The wise man, in doing one thing, does all; or, in the one thing he does rightly, he sees the likeness of all which is done rightly."

Words and actions are not the attributes of brute nature. They introduce us to the human form, of which all other organizations appear to be degradations. When this appears among so many that surround it, the spirit prefers it to all others. It says, 'From such as this, have I drawn joy and knowledge; in such as this, have I found and beheld myself; I will speak to it; it can speak again; it can yield me thought already formed and alive.' In fact, the eye, —the mind, —is always accompanied by these forms, male and female; and these are incomparably the richest informations of the power and order that lie at the heart of things. Unfortunately, every one of them bears the marks as of some injury; is marred and superficially defective. Nevertheless, far different from the deaf and dumb nature around them, these all rest like fountain-pipes on the unfathomed sea of thought and virtue whereto they alone, of all organizations, are the entrances.

It were a pleasant inquiry to follow into detail their ministry to our education, but where would it stop? We are associated in adolescent and adult life with some friends, who, like skies and waters, are coextensive with our idea; who, answering each to a certain affection of the soul, satisfy our desire on that side; whom we lack power to put at such focal distance from us, that we can mend or even analyze them. We cannot choose but love them. When much intercourse with a friend has supplied us with a standard of excellence, and has increased our respect for the resources of God who thus sends a real person to outgo our ideal; when he has, moreover, become an object of thought, and, whilst his character retains all its unconscious effect, is converted in the mind into solid and sweet wisdom,—it is a sign to us that his office is closing, and he is commonly withdrawn from our sight in a short time.

Chapter VI: Idealism

Thus is the unspeakable but intelligible and practicable meaning of the world conveyed to man, the immortal pupil, in every object of sense. To this one end of Discipline, all parts of nature conspire.

A noble doubt perpetually suggests itself, whether this end be not the Final Cause of the Universe; and whether nature outwardly exists. It is a sufficient account of that Appearance we call the World, that God will teach a human mind, and so makes it the receiver of a certain number of congruent sensations, which we call sun and moon, man and woman, house and trade. In my utter impotence to test the authenticity of the report of my senses, to know whether the impressions they make on me correspond with outlying objects, what difference does it make, whether Orion is up there in heaven, or some god paints the image in the firmament of the soul? The relations of parts and the end of the whole remaining the same, what is the difference, whether land and sea interact, and worlds revolve and intermingle without number or end,—deep yawning under deep, and galaxy balancing galaxy, throughout absolute space,—or, whether, without relations of time and space, the same appearances are inscribed in the constant faith of man? Whether nature enjoy a substantial existence without, or is only in the apocalypse of the mind, it is alike useful and alike venerable to me. Be it what it may, it is ideal to me, so long as I cannot try the accuracy of my senses.

The frivolous make themselves merry with the Ideal theory, if its consequences were burlesque; as if it affected the stability of nature. It surely does not. God never jests with us, and will not compromise the end of nature, by permitting any inconsequence in its procession. Any distrust of the permanence of laws, would paralyze the faculties of man. Their permanence is sacredly respected, and his faith therein is perfect. The wheels and springs of man are all set to the hypothesis of the permanence of nature. We are not built like a ship to be tossed, but like a house to stand. It is a natural consequence of this structure, that, so long as the active powers predominate over the reflective, we resist with indignation any hint that nature is more short-lived or mutable than spirit. The broker, the wheelwright, the carpenter, the toll-man, are much displeased at the intimation.

But whilst we acquiesce entirely in the permanence of natural laws, the question of the absolute existence of nature still remains open. It is the uniform effect of culture on the human mind, not to shake our faith in the stability of particular phenomena, as of heat, water, azote; but to lead us to regard nature as a phenomenon, not a substance; to attribute necessary existence to spirit; to esteem nature as an accident and an effect.

To the senses and the unrenewed understanding, belongs a sort of instinctive belief in the absolute existence of nature. In their view, man and nature are indissolubly joined. Things are ultimates, and they never look beyond their sphere. The presence of Reason mars this faith. The first effort of thought tends to relax this despotism of the senses, which binds us to nature as if we were a part of it, and shows us nature aloof, and, as it were, afloat. Until this higher agency intervened, the animal eye sees, with wonderful accuracy, sharp outlines and colored surfaces. When the eye of Reason opens, to outline and surface are at once added, grace and expression. These proceed from imagination and affection and abate somewhat of the angular distinctness of objects. If the Reason be stimulated to more earnest vision, outlines and surfaces become transparent and are no longer seen; causes and spirits are seen through them. The best moments of life are these delicious awakenings of the higher powers, and the reverential withdrawing of nature before its God.

Let us proceed to indicate the effects of culture.

1. Our first institution in the Ideal philosophy is a hint from nature herself.

Nature is made to conspire with spirit to emancipate us. Certain mechanical changes, a small alteration in our local position apprizes us of a dualism. We are strangely affected by seeing the shore from a moving ship, from a balloon, or through the tints of an unusual sky. The least change in our point of view gives the whole world a pictorial air. A man who seldom rides, needs only to get into a coach and traverse his own town, to turn the street into a puppet-show. The men, the women, —talking, running, bartering, fighting, —the earnest mechanic, the lounger, the beggar, the boys, the dogs, are unrealized at once, or, at least, wholly detached from all relation to the observer, and seen as apparent, not substantial beings. What new thoughts are suggested by seeing a face of country quite familiar, in the rapid movement of the rail-road car! Nay, the most wonted objects, (make a very slight change in the point of vision,) please us most. In a camera obscura, the butcher's cart, and the figure of one of our own family amuse us. So, a portrait of a well-known face gratifies us. Turn the eyes upside down, by looking at the landscape through your legs, and how agreeable is the picture, though you have seen it any time these twenty years!

In these cases, by mechanical means, is suggested the difference between the observer and the spectacle, —between man and nature. Hence arises a pleasure mixed with awe; I may say, a low degree of the sublime is felt from the fact, probably, that man is hereby apprized, that, whilst the world is a spectacle, something in himself is stable.

2. In a higher manner, the poet communicates the same pleasure. By a few strokes he delineates, as on air, the sun, the mountain, the camp, the city, the hero, the maiden, not different from what we know them, but only lifted from the ground and afloat before the eye. He unfixes the land and the sea, makes them revolve around the axis of his primary thought, and disposes them anew. Possessed himself by a heroic passion, he uses matter as symbols of it. The sensual man conforms thoughts to things; the poet conforms things to his thoughts. The one esteems nature as rooted and fast; the other, as fluid, and impresses his being thereon. To him, the refractory world is ductile and flexible; he invests dust and stones with humanity, and makes them the words of the Reason. The Imagination may be defined to be the use which the Reason makes of the material world. Shakespeare possesses the power of subordinating nature for the purposes of expression, beyond all poets. His imperial muse tosses the creation like a bauble from hand to

hand and uses it to embody any caprice of thought that is upper-most in his mind. The remotest spaces of nature are visited, and the farthest sundered things are brought together, by a subtle spiritual connection. We are made aware that magnitude of material things is relative, and all objects shrink and expand to serve the passion of the poet. Thus, in his sonnets, the lays of birds, the scents and dyes of flowers, he finds to be the shadow of his beloved; time, which keeps her from him, is his chest; the suspicion she has awakened, is her ornament;

The ornament of beauty is Suspect,
A crow which flies in heaven's sweetest air.

His passion is not the fruit of chance; it swells, as he speaks, to a city, or a state.

No, it was builded far from accident;
It suffers not in smiling pomp, nor falls
Under the brow of thralling discontent;
That works on leases of short numbered hours,
But all alone stands hugely politic.

In the strength of his constancy, the Pyramids seem to him recent and transitory. The freshness of youth and love dazzles him with its resemblance to morning.

Take those lips away
Which so sweetly were forsworn;
And those eyes, —the break of day,
Lights that do mislead the morn.

The wild beauty of this hyperbole, I may say, in passing, it would not be easy to match in literature.

This transfiguration which all material objects undergo through the passion of the poet, —this power which he exerts to dwarf the great, to magnify the small, —might be illustrated by a thousand examples from his Plays. I have before me the Tempest and will cite only these few lines.

Ariel. The strong based promontory
Have I made shake, and by the spurs plucked up
The pine and cedar.

Prospero calls for music to soothe the frantic Alonzo, and his companions;

A solemn air, and the best comforter
To an unsettled fancy, cure thy brains
Now useless, boiled within thy skull.

Again;

The charm dissolves apace,
And, as the morning steals upon the night,
Melting the darkness, so their rising senses
Begin to chase the ignorant fumes that mantle
Their clearer reason.
Their understanding
Begins to swell: and the approaching tide
Will shortly fill the reasonable shores
That now lie foul and muddy.

The perception of real affinities between events, (that is to say, of ideal affinities, for those only are real), enables the poet thus to make free with the most imposing forms and phenomena of the world, and to assert the predominance of the soul.

3. Whilst thus the poet animates nature with his own thoughts, he differs from the philosopher only herein, that the one proposes Beauty as his main end; the other Truth. But the philosopher, not less than the poet, postpones the apparent order and relations of things to the empire of thought. "The problem of philosophy," according to Plato, "is, for all that exists conditionally, to find a ground unconditioned and absolute." It proceeds on the faith that a law determines all phenomena, which being known, the phenomena can be predicted. That law, when in the mind, is an idea. Its beauty is infinite. The true philosopher and

the true poet are one, and a beauty, which is truth, and a truth, which is beauty, is the aim of both. Is not the charm of one of Plato's or Aristotle's definitions, strictly like that of the Antigone of Sophocles? It is, in both cases, that a spiritual life has been imparted to nature; that the solid seeming block of matter has been pervaded and dissolved by a thought; that this feeble human being has penetrated the vast masses of nature with an informing soul, and recognised itself in their harmony, that is, seized their law. In physics, when this is attained, the memory disburthens itself of its cumbrous catalogues of particulars, and carries centuries of observation in a single formula.

Thus even in physics, the material is degraded before the spiritual. The astronomer, the geometer, rely on their irrefragable analysis, and disdain the results of observation. The sublime remark of Euler on his law of arches, "This will be found contrary to all experience, yet is true;" had already transferred nature into the mind, and left matter like an outcast corpse.

4. Intellectual science has been observed to beget invariably a doubt of the existence of matter. Turgot said, "He that has never doubted the existence of matter, may be assured he has no aptitude for metaphysical inquiries." It fastens the attention upon immortal necessary uncreated natures, that is, upon Ideas; and in their presence, we feel that the outward circumstance is a dream and a shade. Whilst we wait in this Olympus of gods, we think of nature as an appendix to the soul. We ascend into their region and know that these are the thoughts of the Supreme Being. "These are they who were set up from everlasting, from the beginning, or ever the earth was. When he prepared the heavens, they were there; when he established the clouds above, when he strengthened the fountains of the deep. Then they were by him, as one brought up with him. Of them took he counsel."

Their influence is proportionate. As objects of science, they are accessible to few men. Yet all men are capable of being raised by piety or by passion, into their region. And no man touches these divine natures, without becoming, in some degree, himself divine. Like a new soul, they renew the body. We become physically nimble and lightsome; we tread on air; life is no longer irksome, and we think it will never be so. No man fears age or misfortune or death, in their serene company, for he is transported out of the district of change. Whilst we behold unveiled the nature of Justice and Truth, we learn the difference between the absolute and the conditional or relative. We apprehend the absolute. As it were, for the first time, we exist. We become immortal, for we learn that time and space are relations of matter; that, with a perception of truth, or a virtuous will, they have no affinity.

5. Finally, religion and ethics, which may be fitly called, the practice of ideas, or the introduction of ideas into life, have an analogous effect with all lower culture, in degrading nature and suggesting its dependence on spirit. Ethics and religion differ herein; that the one is the system of human duties commencing from man; the other, from God. Religion includes the personality of God; Ethics does not. They are one to our present design. They both put nature under foot. The first and last lesson of religion is, "The things that are seen are temporal; the things that are unseen, are eternal." It puts an affront upon nature. It does that for the unschooled, which philosophy does for Berkeley and Viasa. The uniform language that may be heard in the churches of the most ignorant sects, is, "Contemn the unsubstantial shows of the world; they are vanities, dreams, shadows, unrealities; seek the realities of religion." The devotee flouts nature. Some theosophists have arrived at a certain hostility and indignation towards matter, as the Manichean and Plotinus. They distrusted in themselves any looking back to these flesh-pots of Egypt. Plotinus was ashamed of his body. In short, they might all say of matter, what Michael Angelo said of external beauty, "it is the frail and weary weed, in which God dresses the soul, which he has called into time."

It appears that motion, poetry, physical and intellectual science, and religion, all tend to affect our convictions of the reality of the external world. But I own there is something ungrateful in expanding too curiously the particulars of the general proposition, that all culture tends to imbue us with idealism. I have no hostility to nature, but a child's love to it. I expand and live in the warm day like corn and melons. Let us speak her fair. I do not wish to fling stones at my beautiful mother, nor soil my gentle nest. I only wish to indicate the true position of nature in regard to man, wherein to establish man, all right education tends; as the ground which to attain is the object of human life, that is, of man's connection with nature. Culture inverts the vulgar views of nature, and brings the mind to call that apparent, which it uses to call real, and that real, which it uses to call visionary. Children, it is true, believe in the external world. The belief that it appears only, is an afterthought, but with culture, this faith will as surely arise on the mind as did the first.

The advantage of the ideal theory over the popular faith, is this, that it presents the world in precisely that view which is most desirable to the mind. It is, in fact, the view which Reason, both speculative and practical, that is, philosophy and virtue, take. For, seen in the light of thought, the world always is phenomenal; and virtue subordinates it to the mind. Idealism sees the world in God. It beholds the whole circle of persons and things, of actions and events, of country and religion, not as painfully accumulated, atom after atom, act after act, in an aged creeping Past, but as one vast picture, which God paints on the instant eternity, for the contemplation of the soul. Therefore the soul holds itself off from a too trivial and microscopic study of the universal tablet. It respects the end too much, to immerse itself in the means. It sees something more important in Christianity, than the scandals of ecclesiastical history, or the niceties of criticism; and very incurious concerning persons or miracles, and not at all disturbed by chasms of historical evidence, it accepts from God the phenomenon, as it finds it, as the pure and awful form of religion in the world. It is not hot and passionate at the appearance of what it calls its own good or bad fortune, at the union or opposition of other persons. No man is its enemy. It accepts whatsoever befalls, as part of its lesson. It is a watcher more than a doer, and it is a doer, only that it may the better watch.

Chapter VII: Spirit

It is essential to a true theory of nature and of man, that it should contain somewhat progressive. Uses that are exhausted or that may be, and facts that end in the statement, cannot be all that is true of this brave lodging wherein man is harbored, and wherein all his faculties find appropriate and endless exercise. And all the uses of nature admit of being summed in one, which yields the activity of man an infinite scope. Through all its kingdoms, to the suburbs and outskirts of things, it is faithful to the cause whence it had its origin. It always speaks of Spirit. It suggests the absolute. It is a perpetual effect. It is a great shadow pointing always to the sun behind us.

The aspect of nature is devout. Like the figure of Jesus, she stands with bended head, and hands folded upon the breast. The happiest man is he who learns from nature the lesson of worship.

Of that ineffable essence which we call Spirit, he that thinks most, will say least. We can foresee God in the coarse, and, as it were, distant phenomena of matter; but when we try to define and describe himself, both language and thought desert us, and we are as helpless as fools and savages. That essence refuses to be recorded in propositions, but when man has worshipped him intellectually, the noblest ministry of nature is to stand as the apparition of God. It is the organ through which the universal spirit speaks to the individual and strives to lead back the individual to it.

When we consider Spirit, we see that the views already presented do not include the whole circumference of man. We must add some related thoughts.

Three problems are put by nature to the mind; What is matter? Whence is it? and Whereto? The first of these questions only, the ideal theory answers. Idealism saith: matter is a phenomenon, not a substance. Idealism acquaints us with the total disparity between the evidence of our own being, and the evidence of the world's being. The one is perfect; the other, incapable of any assurance; the mind is a part of the nature of things; the world is a divine dream, from which we may presently awake to the glories and certainties of day. Idealism is a hypothesis to account for nature by other principles than those of carpentry and chemistry. Yet, if it only deny the existence of matter, it does not satisfy the demands of the spirit. It leaves God out of me. It leaves me in the splendid labyrinth of my perceptions, to wander without end. Then the heart resists it, because it balks the affections in denying substantive being to men and women. Nature is so pervaded with human life, that there is something of humanity in all, and in every particular. But this theory makes nature foreign to me and does not account for that consanguinity which we acknowledge to it.

Let it stand, then, in the present state of our knowledge, merely as a useful introductory hypothesis, serving to apprize us of the eternal distinction between the soul and the world.

But when, following the invisible steps of thought, we come to inquire, Whence is matter? and Whereto? many truths arise to us out of the recesses of consciousness. We learn that the highest is present to the soul of man, that the dread universal essence, which is not wisdom, or love, or beauty, or power, but all in one, and each entirely, is that for which all things exist, and that by which they are; that spirit creates; that behind nature, throughout nature, spirit is present; one and not compound, it does not act upon us from without, that is, in space and time, but spiritually, or through ourselves: therefore, that spirit, that is, the Supreme Being, does not build up nature around us, but puts it forth through us, as the life of the tree puts forth new branches and leaves through the pores of the old. As a plant upon the earth, so a man rests upon the bosom of God; he is nourished by unfailing fountains, and draws, at his need, inexhaustible power. Who can set bounds to the possibilities of man? Once inhale the upper air, being admitted to behold the absolute natures of justice and truth, and we learn that man has access to the entire mind of the Creator, is himself the creator in the finite. This view, which admonishes me where the sources of wisdom and power lie, and points to virtue as to carries upon its face the highest certificate of truth, because it animates me to create my own world through the purification of my soul.

"The golden key
Which opes the palace of eternity,"

The world proceeds from the same spirit as the body of man. It is a remoter and inferior incarnation of God, a projection of God in the unconscious. But it differs from the body in one important respect. It is not, like that, now subjected to the human will. Its serene order is inviolable by us. It is, therefore, to us, the present expositor of the divine mind. It is a fixed point whereby we may measure our departure. As we degenerate, the contrast between us and our house is more evident. We are as much strangers in nature, as we are aliens from God. We do not understand the notes of birds. The fox and the deer run away from us; the bear and tiger rend us. We do not know the uses of more than a few plants, as corn and the apple, the potato and the vine. Is not the landscape, every glimpse of which hath a grandeur, a face of him? Yet this may show us what discord is between man and nature, for you cannot freely admire a noble landscape, if laborers are digging in the field hard by. The poet finds something ridiculous in his delight, until he is out of the sight of men.

Chapter VIII: Prospects

In inquiries respecting the laws of the world and the frame of things, the highest reason is always the truest. That which seems faintly possible is so refined, is often faint and dim because it is deepest seated in the mind among the eternal verities. Empirical science is apt to cloud the sight, and, by the very knowledge of functions and processes, to bereave the student of the manly contemplation of the whole. The savant becomes unpoetic. But the best read naturalist who lends an entire and devout attention to truth, will see that there remains much to learn of his relation to the world, and that it is not to be learned by any addition or subtraction or other comparison of known quantities, but is arrived at by untaught sallies of the spirit, by a continual self-recovery, and by entire humility. He will perceive that there are far more excellent qualities in the student than preciseness and infallibility; that a guess is often more fruitful than an indisputable affirmation, and that a dream may let us deeper into the secret of nature than a hundred concerted experiments.

For, the problems to be solved are precisely those which the physiologist and the naturalist omit to state. It is not so pertinent to man to know all the individuals of the animal kingdom, as it is to know whence and whereto is this tyrannizing unity in his constitution, which evermore separates and classifies things, endeavoring to reduce the most diverse to one form. When I behold a rich landscape, it is less to my purpose to recite correctly the order and superposition of the strata, than to know why all thought of multitude is lost in a tranquil sense of unity. I cannot greatly honor minuteness in details, so long as there is no hint to explain the relation between things and thoughts; no ray upon the *metaphysics* of conchology, of botany, of the arts, to show the relation of the forms of flowers, shells, animals, architecture, to the mind, and build science upon ideas. In a cabinet of natural history, we become sensible of a certain occult recognition and sympathy in regard to the most unwieldly and eccentric forms of beast, fish, and insect. The American who has been confined, in his own country, to the sight of buildings designed after foreign models, is surprised on entering York Minster or St. Peter's at Rome, by the feeling that these structures are imitations also, —faint copies of an invisible archetype. Nor has science sufficient humanity, so long as the naturalist overlooks that wonderful congruity which subsists between man and the world; of which he is lord, not because he is the most subtile inhabitant, but because he is its head and heart, and finds something of himself in every great and small thing, in every mountain stratum, in every new law of color, fact of astronomy, or atmospheric influence which observation or analysis lay open. A perception of this mystery inspires the muse of George Herbert, the beautiful psalmist of the seventeenth century. The following lines are part of his little poem on Man.

'Man is all symmetry,
Full of proportions, one limb to another,
And to all the world besides.
Each part may call the farthest, brother;
For head with foot hath private amity,
And both with moons and tides.

'Nothing hath got so far
But man hath caught and kept it as his prey;
His eyes dismount the highest star;
He is in little all the sphere.
Herbs gladly cure our flesh, because that they
Find their acquaintance there.

'For us, the winds do blow,
The earth doth rest, heaven move, and fountains flow;
Nothing we see, but means our good,
As our delight, or as our treasure;
The whole is either our cupboard of food,
Or cabinet of pleasure.

"The stars have us to bed:
Night draws the curtain; which the sun withdraws.
Music and light attend our head.
All things unto our flesh are kind,
In their descent and being; to our mind,
In their ascent and cause.

"More servants wait on man
Than he'll take notice of. In every path,
He treads down that which doth befriend him
When sickness makes him pale and wan.
Oh mighty love! Man is one world, and hath
Another to attend him."

The perception of this class of truths makes the attraction which draws men to science, but the end is lost sight of in attention to the means. In view of this half-sight of science, we accept the sentence of Plato, that, "poetry comes nearer to vital truth than history." Every surmise and vaticination of the mind is entitled to a certain respect, and we learn to prefer imperfect theories, and sentences, which contain glimpses of truth, to digested systems which have no one valuable suggestion. A wise writer will feel that the ends of study and composition are best answered by announcing undiscovered regions of thought, and so communicating, through hope, new activity to the torpid spirit.

I shall therefore conclude this essay with some traditions of man and nature, which a certain poet sang to me; and which, as they have always been in the world, and perhaps reappear to every bard, may be both history and prophecy.

'The foundations of man are not in matter, but in spirit. But the element of spirit is eternity. To it, therefore, the longest series of events, the oldest chronologies are young and recent. In the cycle of the universal man, from whom the known individuals proceed, centuries are points, and all history is but the epoch of one degradation.

'We distrust and deny inwardly our sympathy with nature. We own and disown our relation to it, by turns. We are, like Nebuchadnezzar, dethroned, bereft of reason, and eating grass like an ox. But who can set limits to the remedial force of spirit?

'A man is a god in ruins. When men are innocent, life shall be longer, and shall pass into the immortal, as gently as we awake from dreams. Now, the world would be insane and rabid, if these disorganizations should last for hundreds of years. It is kept in check by death and infancy. Infancy is the perpetual Messiah, which comes into the arms of fallen men, and pleads with them to return to paradise.

'Man is the dwarf of himself. Once he was permeated and dissolved by spirit. He filled nature with his overflowing currents. Out from him sprang the sun and moon; from man, the sun; from woman, the moon. The laws of his mind, the periods of his actions externized themselves into day and night, into the year and the seasons. But, having made for himself this huge shell, his waters retired; he no longer fills the veins and veinlets; he is shrunk to a drop. He sees, that the structure still fits him, but fits him colossally. Say, rather, once it fitted him, now it corresponds to him from far and on high. He adores timidly his own work. Now is man the follower of the sun, and woman the follower of the moon. Yet sometimes he starts in his slumber, and wonders at himself and his house, and muses strangely at the resemblance betwixt him and it. He perceives that if his law is still paramount, if still he have elemental power, if his word is sterling yet in nature, it is not conscious power, it is not inferior but superior to his will. It is Instinct.' Thus my Orphic poet sang.

At present, man applies to nature but half his force. He works on the world with his understanding alone. He lives in it, and masters it by a penny-wisdom; and he that works most in it, is but a half-man, and whilst his arms are strong and his digestion good, his mind is imbruted, and he is a selfish savage. His relation to nature, his power over it, is through the understanding; as by manure; the economic use of fire, wind, water, and the mariner's needle; steam, coal, chemical agriculture; the repairs of the human body by the dentist and the surgeon. This is such a resumption of power, as if a banished king should buy his territories inch by inch, instead of vaulting at once into his throne. Meantime, in the thick darkness, there are not wanting gleams of a better light, —occasional examples of the action of man upon nature with his entire force, —with reason as well as understanding. Such examples are; the traditions of miracles in the earliest antiquity of all nations; the history of Jesus Christ; the achievements of a principle, as in religious and political revolutions, and in the abolition of the Slave-trade; the miracles of enthusiasm, as those reported of Swedenborg, Hohenlohe, and the Shakers; many obscure and yet contested facts, now arranged under the name of Animal Magnetism; prayer; eloquence; self-healing; and the wisdom of children. These are examples of Reason's momentary grasp of the sceptre; the exertions of a power which exists not in time or space, but an instantaneous in-streaming causing power. The difference between the actual and the ideal force of man is happily figured by the schoolmen, in saying, that the knowledge of man is an evening knowledge, vespertina cognitio, but that of God is a morning knowledge, matutina cognitio.

The problem of restoring to the world original and eternal beauty, is solved by the redemption of the soul. The ruin or the blank that we see when we look at nature, is in our own eye. The axis of vision is not coincident with the axis of things, and so they appear not transparent but opake. The reason why the world lacks unity, and lies broken and in heaps, is, because man is disunited with himself. He cannot be a naturalist, until he satisfies all the demands of the spirit. Love is as much its demand, as perception. Indeed, neither can be perfect without the other. In the uttermost meaning of the words, thought is devout, and devotion is thought. Deep calls unto deep. But in actual life, the marriage is not celebrated. There are innocent men who worship God after the tradition of their fathers, but their sense of duty has not yet extended to the use of all their faculties. And there are patient naturalists, but they freeze their subject under the wintry light of the understanding. Is not prayer also a study of truth,—a sally of the soul into the unfound infinite? No man ever prayed heartily, without learning something. But when a faithful thinker, resolute to detach every object from personal relations, and see it in the light of thought, shall, at the same time, kindle science with the fire of the holiest affections, then will God go forth anew into the creation.

It will not need, when the mind is prepared for study, to search for objects. The invariable mark of wisdom is to see the miraculous in the common. What is a day? What is a year? What is summer? What is woman? What is a child? What is sleep? To our blindness, these things seem unaffecting. We make fables to hide the baldness of the fact and conform it, as we say, to the higher law of the mind. But when the fact is seen under the light of an idea, the gaudy fable fades and shrivels. We behold the real higher law. To the wise, therefore, a fact is true poetry, and the most beautiful of fables. These wonders are brought to our own door. You also are a man. Man and woman, and their social life, poverty, labor, sleep, fear, fortune, are known to you. Learn that none of these things is superficial, but that each phenomenon has its roots in the faculties and affections of the mind. Whilst the abstract question occupies your intellect, nature brings it in the concrete to be solved by your hands. It were a wise inquiry for the closet, to compare, point by point, especially at remarkable crises in life, our daily history, with the rise and progress of ideas in the mind.

So shall we come to look at the world with new eyes. It shall answer the endless inquiry of the intellect,—What is truth? and of the affections,—What is good? by yielding itself passive to the educated Will. Then shall come to pass what my poet said; 'Nature is not fixed but fluid. Spirit alters, moulds, makes it. The immobility or bruteness of nature, is the absence of spirit; to pure spirit, it is fluid, it is volatile, it is obedient. Every spirit builds itself a house; and beyond its house a world; and beyond its world, a heaven. Know then, that the world exists for you. For you is the phenomenon perfect. What we are, that only can we see. All that Adam had, all that Caesar could, you have and can do. Adam called his house, heaven and earth; Caesar called his house, Rome; you perhaps call yours, a cobler's trade; a hundred acres of ploughed land; or a scholar's garret. Yet line for line and point for point, your dominion is as great as theirs, though without fine names. Build, therefore, your own world. As fast as you conform your life to the pure idea in your mind, that will unfold its great proportions. A correspondent revolution in things will attend the influx of the spirit. So fast will disagreeable appearances, swine, spiders, snakes, pests, madhouses, prisons, enemies, vanish; they are temporary and shall be no more seen. The sordor and filths of nature, the sun shall dry up, and the wind exhale. As when the summer comes from the south; the snow-banks melt, and the face of the earth becomes green before it, so shall the advancing spirit create its ornaments along its path, and carry with it the beauty it visits, and the song which enchants it; it shall draw beautiful faces, warm hearts, wise discourse, and heroic acts, around its way, until evil is no more seen. The kingdom of man over nature, which cometh not with observation, —a dominion such as now is beyond his dream of God, —he shall enter without more wonder than the blind man feels who is gradually restored to perfect sight.'

Henry David Thoreau (1817–62)

Born July 12th in 1817, Henry David Thoreau was the third child of John Thoreau, a pencil manufacturer, and Cynthia Dunbar, who rented out parts of their home. Despite moving out of his hometown of Concord, Massachusetts in 1818, the family returned to Concord in 1823 where Thoreau stayed until he left for Harvard University in 1833. There he studied Greek, Latin, and German and used the school library frequently. After graduating in 1837, Thoreau began teaching at his childhood Concord grammar school but was not fond of being a disciplinarian, so he quit after two weeks. Still wanting to teach, he and his brother, John Thoreau, started a small school in 1838. The school seemed successful until John died from tetanus having cut himself shaving four years later, forcing Thoreau to shut down the school.

During his teaching career, Thoreau began his friendship with Ralph Waldo Emerson. At Emerson's suggestion, Thoreau began journaling in 1837. In 1839 after a canoe trip along the Concord and Merrimack rivers with John, Thoreau felt more inclined to be a poet of nature rather than a schoolmaster. After the closing of his school, Thoreau formally took on the title of "poet."

In the 1840s, he helped Emerson's magazine, The Dial, which published many of his poems including "Sympathy." In 1842, Thoreau wrote his first outdoors essay, "Natural History of Massachusetts." During this time, Thoreau stayed at Emerson's home, working on more literature and acting as a caretaker. Grief from the death of his brother John in 1842 added to the restlessness that Thoreau felt in the Emerson home. Thoreau went to New York to tutor in the Staten

Island household of Emerson's brother, William Emerson, but Thoreau had a strong distaste for city life and returned to Concord less than a year later. Thoreau began writing more about the outdoors in works such as "A Winter Walk" (1843) due to his love for the wilderness compared to the city.

Thoreau began seeking a simpler life, so after building his home on Walden Pond in 1845, he moved his whole life to his new cabin. The satisfaction he received while chopping the pine trees down for his home and growing his own food cured his previous restlessness. He experimented with working as little as possible and as hard as possible to switch up his routine. He observed the animals in the area and journaled his findings. Later, he revised his journals and essays to produce *Walden* (1854). *Walden* provides his perspective on living as self-sufficiently as possible and the intimacy he had with the creatures at the pond. Thoreau left Walden Pond after an invitation from Emerson to stay with Emerson's wife and children while he himself went the Europe.

Thoreau became a surveyor, or a professional that measures and maps landscapes, in his later years. He collected botanical and reptilian specimens for both his own research and the collection at Harvard. He travelled during his surveyor years to gain personal experience his published works in magazines, like "Excursion to Canada" in *Putnam's Monthly* (1853) and "Cape Cod," in *Putnam's* (1855). These articles showed his appreciation for natural environments and adventure.

Thoreau spent the rest of his life more as an activist than a Transcendentalist. During his stay at Walden Pond, Thoreau spent a night in jail for refusing to pay his poll tax. This experience deepened his distaste for the government. After leaving Walden Pond, he wrote "Civil Disobedience" (1849)—originally titled "Resistance to Civil Government." He could not support a government that sanctioned slavery. He wrote more against slavery with his lecture, "Slavery in Massachusetts" in 1854. Thoreau met John Brown, an abolitionist, who replaced the father figure that Emerson once was to him. Thoreau delivered "A Plea for Captain John Brown" after the raid on Harpers Ferry that caused Brown's imprisonment. The shock from witnessing Brown's hanging in 1859 worsened Thoreau's health, leading to his death in 1862 after contracting tuberculosis.

Excerpts from

WALDEN

By Henry David Thoreau

II
Where I Lived, and What I Lived For

At a certain season of our life we are accustomed to consider every spot as the possible site of a house. I have thus surveyed the country on every side within a dozen miles of where I live. In imagination I have bought all the farms in succession, for all were to be bought, and I knew their price. I walked over each farmer's premises, tasted his wild apples, discoursed on husbandry with him, took his farm at his price, at any price, mortgaging it to him in my mind; even put a higher price on it — took everything but a deed of it — took his word for his deed, for I dearly love to talk — cultivated it, and him too to some extent, I trust, and withdrew when I had enjoyed it long enough, leaving him to carry it on. This experience entitled me to be regarded as a sort of real-estate broker by my friends. Wherever I sat, there I might live, and the landscape radiated from me accordingly. What is a house but a *sedes*, a seat? — better if a country seat. I discovered many a site for a house not likely to be soon improved, which some might have thought too far from the village, but to my eyes the village was too far from it. Well, there I might live, I said; and there I did live, for an hour, a summer and a winter life; saw how I could let the years run off, buffet the winter through, and see the spring come in. The future inhabitants of this region, wherever they may place their houses, may be sure that they have been anticipated. An afternoon sufficed to lay out the land into orchard, wood-lot, and pasture, and to decide what fine oaks or pines should be left to stand before the door, and whence each blasted tree could be seen to the best advantage; and then I let it lie, fallow, perchance, for a man is rich in proportion to the number of things which he can afford to let alone.

My imagination carried me so far that I even had the refusal of several farms — the refusal was all I wanted — but I never got my fingers burned by actual possession. The nearest that I came to actual possession was when I bought the Hollowell place, and had begun to sort my seeds, and collected materials with which to make a wheelbarrow to carry it on or off with; but before the owner gave me a deed of it, his wife -- every man has such a wife -- changed her mind and wished to keep it, and he offered me ten dollars to release him. Now, to speak the truth, I had but ten cents in the world, and it surpassed my arithmetic to tell, if I was that man who had ten cents, or who had a farm, or ten dollars, or all together. However, I let him keep the ten dollars and the farm too, for I had carried it far enough; or rather, to be generous, I sold him the farm for just what I gave for it, and, as he was not a rich man, made him a present of ten dollars, and still had my ten cents, and seeds, and materials for a wheelbarrow left. I found thus that I had been a rich man without any damage to my poverty. But I retained the landscape, and I have since annually carried off what it yielded without a wheelbarrow. With respect to landscapes,

> *"I am monarch of all I survey,*
> *My right there is none to dispute."*

I have frequently seen a poet withdraw, having enjoyed the most valuable part of a farm, while the crusty farmer supposed that he had got a few wild apples only. Why, the owner does not know it for many years when a poet has put his farm in rhyme, the most admirable kind of invisible fence, has fairly impounded it, milked it, skimmed it, and got all the cream, and left the farmer only the skimmed milk.

The real attractions of the Hollowell farm, to me, were: its complete retirement, being, about two miles from the village, half a mile from the nearest neighbor, and separated from the highway by a broad field; its bounding on the river, which the owner said protected it by its fogs from frosts in the spring, though that was nothing to me; the gray color and ruinous state of the house and barn, and the dilapidated fences, which put such an interval between me and the last occupant; the hollow and lichen-covered apple trees, nawed by rabbits, showing what kind of neighbors I should have; but above all, the recollection I had of it from my earliest voyages up the river, when the house was concealed behind a dense grove of red maples, through which I heard the house-dog bark. I was in haste to buy it, before the proprietor finished getting out some rocks, cutting down the hollow apple trees, and grubbing up some young birches which had sprung up in the pasture, or, in short, had made any more of his improvements. To enjoy these advantages I was ready to carry it on; like Atlas, to take the world on my shoulders -- I never heard what compensation he received for that — and do all those things which had no other motive or excuse but that I might pay for it and be unmolested in my possession of it; for I knew all the while that it would yield the most abundant crop of the kind I wanted, if I could only afford to let it alone. But it turned out as I have said.

All that I could say, then, with respect to farming on a large scale — I have always cultivated a garden — was, that I had my seeds ready. Many think that seeds improve with age. I have no doubt that time discriminates between the good and the bad; and when at last I shall plant, I shall be less likely to be disappointed. But I would say to my fellows, once for all, As long as possible live free and uncommitted. It makes but little difference whether you are committed to a farm or the county jail.

Old Cato, whose "De Re Rustica" is my "Cultivator," says -- and the only translation I have seen makes sheer nonsense of the passage -- "When you think of getting a farm turn it thus in your mind, not to buy greedily; nor spare your pains to look at it, and do not think it enough to go round it once. The oftener you go there the more it will please you, if it is good." I think I shall not buy greedily, but go round and round it as long as I live, and be buried in it first, that it may please me the more at last.

* * *

The present was my next experiment of this kind, which I purpose to describe more at length, for convenience putting the experience of two years into one. As I have said, I do not propose to write an ode to dejection, but to brag as lustily as chanticleer in the morning, standing on his roost, if only to wake my neighbors up.

When first I took up my abode in the woods, that is, began to spend my nights as well as days there, which, by accident, was on Independence Day, or the Fourth of July, 1845, my house was not finished for winter, but was merely a defence against the rain, without plastering or chimney, the walls being of rough, weather-stained boards, with wide chinks, which made it cool at night. The upright white hewn studs and freshly planed door and window casings gave it a clean and airy look, especially in the morning, when its timbers were saturated with dew, so that I fancied that by noon some sweet gum would exude from them. To my imagination it retained throughout the day more or less of this auroral character, reminding me of a certain house on a mountain which I had visited a year before. This was an airy and unplastered cabin, fit to entertain a travelling god, and where a goddess might trail her garments. The winds which passed over my dwelling were such as sweep over the ridges of mountains, bearing the broken strains, or celestial parts only, of terrestrial music. The morning wind forever blows, the poem of creation is uninterrupted; but few are the ears that hear it. Olympus is but the outside of the earth everywhere.

The only house I had been the owner of before, if I except a boat, was a tent, which I used occasionally when making excursions in the summer, and this is still rolled up in my garret; but the boat, after passing from hand to hand, has gone down the stream of time. With this more substantial shelter about me, I had made some progress toward settling in the world. This frame, so slightly clad, was a sort of crystallization around me, and reacted on the builder. It was suggestive somewhat as a picture in outlines. I did not need to go outdoors to take the air, for the atmosphere within had lost none of its freshness. It was not so much within doors as behind a door where I sat, even in the rainiest weather. The Harivansa says, "An abode without birds is like a meat without seasoning." Such was not my abode, for I found myself suddenly neighbor to the birds; not by having imprisoned one, but having caged myself near them. I was not only nearer to some of those which commonly frequent the garden and the orchard, but to those smaller and more thrilling songsters of the forest which never, or rarely, serenade a villager -- the wood thrush, the veery, the scarlet tanager, the field sparrow, the whip-poor-will, and many others.

I was seated by the shore of a small pond, about a mile and a half south of the village of Concord and somewhat higher than it, in the midst of an extensive wood between that town and Lincoln, and about two miles south of that our only field known to fame, Concord Battle Ground; but I was so low in the woods that the opposite shore, half a mile off, like the rest, covered with wood, was my most distant horizon. For the first week, whenever I looked out on the pond it impressed me like a tarn high up on the side of a mountain, its bottom far above the surface of other lakes, and, as the sun arose, I saw it throwing off its nightly clothing of mist, and here and there, by degrees, its soft ripples or its smooth reflecting surface was revealed, while the mists, like ghosts, were stealthily withdrawing in every direction into the woods, as at the breaking up of some nocturnal conventicle. The very dew seemed to hang upon the trees later into the day than usual, as on the sides of mountains.

This small lake was of most value as a neighbor in the intervals of a gentle rainstorm in August, when, both air and water being perfectly still, but the sky overcast, mid-afternoon had all the serenity of evening, and the wood thrush sang around, and was heard from shore to shore. A lake like this is never smoother than at such a time; and the clear portion of the air above it being, shallow and darkened by clouds, the water, full of light and reflections, becomes a lower heaven itself so much the more important. From a hill-top nearby, where the wood had been recently cut off, there was a pleasing vista southward across the pond, through a wide indentation in the hills which form the shore there, where their opposite sides sloping toward each other suggested a stream flowing out in that direction through a wooded valley, but stream there was none. That way I looked between and over the near green hills to some distant and higher ones in the horizon, tinged with blue. Indeed, by standing on tiptoe I could catch a glimpse of some of the peaks of the still bluer and more distant mountain ranges in the northwest, those true-blue coins from heaven's own mint, and also of some portion of the village. But in other directions, even from this point, I could not see over or beyond the woods which surrounded me. It is well to have some water in your neighborhood, to give buoyancy to and float the earth. One value even of the smallest well is that when you look into it you see that earth is not continent but insular. This is as important as that it keeps butter cool. When I looked across the pond from this peak toward the Sudbury meadows, which in time of flood I distinguished elevated perhaps by a mirage in their seething valley, like a coin in a basin, all the earth beyond the pond appeared like a thin crust insulated and floated even by this small sheet of interverting water, and I was reminded that this on which I dwelt was but *dry land.*

Though the view from my door was still more contracted, I did not feel crowded or confined in the least. There was pasture enough for my imagination. The low shrub oak plateau to which the opposite shore arose stretched away toward the prairies of the West and the steppes of Tartary, affording ample room for all the roving families of men. "There are none happy in the world but beings who enjoy freely a vast horizon," said Damodara, when his herds required new and larger pastures.

Both place and time were changed, and I dwelt nearer to those parts of the universe and to those eras in history which had most attracted me. Where I lived was as far off as many a region viewed nightly by astronomers. We are wont to imagine rare and delectable places in some remote and more celestial corner of the system, behind the constellation of Cassiopeia's Chair, far from noise and disturbance. I discovered that my house actually had its site in such a withdrawn, but forever new and unprofaned, part of the universe. If it were worth the while to settle in those parts near to the Pleiades or the Hyades, to Aldebaran or Altair, then I was really there, or at an equal remoteness from the life which I had left behind, dwindled and twinkling with as fine a ray to my nearest neighbor, and to be seen only in moonless nights by him. Such was that part of creation where I had squatted;

"There was a shepherd that did live,
And held his thoughts as high
As were the mounts whereon his flocks
Did hourly feed him by."

What should we think of the shepherd's life if his flocks always wandered to higher pastures than his thoughts?

Every morning was a cheerful invitation to make my life of equal simplicity, and I may say innocence, with Nature herself. I have been as sincere a worshipper of Aurora as the Greeks. I got up early and bathed in the pond; that was a religious exercise, and one of the best things which I did. They say that characters were engraven on the bathing tub of King Tchingthang to this effect: "Renew thyself completely each day; do it again, and again, and forever again." I can understand that. Morning brings back the heroic ages. I was as much affected by the faint hum of a mosquito making its invisible and unimaginable tour through my apartment at earliest dawn, when I was sitting with door and windows open, as I could be by any trumpet that ever sang of fame. It was Homer's requiem; itself an Iliad and Odyssey in the air, singing its own wrath and wanderings. There was something cosmical about it; a standing advertisement, till forbidden, of the everlasting vigor and fertility of the world. The morning, which is the most memorable season of the day, is the awakening hour. Then there is least somnolence in us; and for an hour, at least, some part of us awakes which slumbers all the rest of the day and night. Little is to be expected of that day, if it can be called a day, to which we are not awakened by our Genius, but by the mechanical nudgings of some servitor, are not awakened by our own newly acquired force and aspirations from within, accompanied by the undulations of celestial music, instead of factory bells, and a fragrance filling the air — to a higher life than we fell asleep from; and thus the darkness bear its fruit, and prove itself to be good, no less than the light. That man who does not believe that each day contains an earlier, more sacred, and auroral hour than he has yet profaned, has despaired of life, and is pursuing a descending and darkening way. After a partial cessation of his sensuous life, the soul of man, or its organs rather, are reinvigorated each day, and his Genius tries again what noble life it can make. All memorable events, I should say, transpire in morning time and in a morning atmosphere. The Vedas say, "All intelligences awake with the morning." Poetry and art, and the fairest and most memorable of the actions of men, date from such an hour. All poets and heroes, like Memnon, are the children of Aurora, and emit their music at sunrise. To him whose elastic and vigorous thought keeps pace with the sun, the day is a perpetual morning. It matters not what the clocks say or the attitudes and labors of men. Morning is when I am awake and there is a dawn in me. Moral reform is the effort to throw off sleep. Why is it that men give so poor an account of their day if they have not been slumbering? They are not such poor calculators. If they had not been overcome with drowsiness, they would have performed something. The millions are awake enough for physical labor; but only one in a million is awake enough for effective intellectual exertion, only one in a hundred millions to a poetic or divine life. To be awake is to be alive. I have never yet met a man who was quite awake. How could I have looked him in the face?

We must learn to reawaken and keep ourselves awake, not by mechanical aids, but by an infinite expectation of the dawn, which does not forsake us in our soundest sleep. I know of no more encouraging fact than the unquestionable ability of man to elevate his life by a conscious endeavor. It is something to be able to paint a particular picture, or to carve a statue, and so to make a few objects beautiful; but it is far more glorious to carve and paint the very atmosphere and medium through which we look, which morally we can do. To affect the quality of the day, that is the highest of arts. Every man is tasked to make his life, even in its details, worthy of the contemplation of his most elevated and critical hour. If we refused, or rather used up, such paltry information as we get, the oracles would distinctly inform us how this might be done.

I went to the woods because I wished to live deliberately, to front only the essential facts of life, and see if I could not learn what it had to teach, and not, when I came to die, discover that I had not lived. I did not wish to live what was not life, living is so dear; nor did I wish to practise resignation, unless it was quite necessary. I wanted to live deep and suck out all the marrow of life, to live so sturdily and Spartan-like as to put to rout all that was not life, to cut a broad swath and shave close, to drive life into a corner, and reduce it to its lowest terms, and, if it proved to be mean, why then to get the whole and genuine meanness of it, and publish its meanness to the world; or if it were sublime, to know it by experience, and be able to give a true account of it in my next excursion. For most men, it appears to me, are in a strange uncertainty about it, whether it is of the devil or of God, and have somewhat *hastily concluded* that it is the chief end of man here to "glorify God and enjoy him forever."

Still we live meanly, like ants; though the fable tells us that we were long ago changed into men; like pygmies we fight with cranes; it is error upon error, and clout upon clout, and our best virtue has for its occasion a superfluous and evitable wretchedness. Our life is frittered away by detail. An honest man has hardly need to count more than his ten fingers, or in extreme cases he may add his ten toes, and lump the rest. Simplicity, simplicity, simplicity! I say, let your affairs be as two or three, and not a hundred or a thousand; instead of a million count half a dozen, and keep your accounts on your thumb-nail. In the midst of this chopping sea of civilized life, such are the clouds and storms and quicksands and thousand-and-one items to be allowed for, that a man has to live, if he would not founder and go to the bottom and not make his port at all, by dead reckoning, and he must be a great calculator indeed who succeeds. Simplify, simplify. Instead of three meals a day, if it be necessary eat but one; instead of a hundred dishes, five; and reduce other things in proportion. Our life is like a German Confederacy, made up of petty states, with its boundary forever fluctuating, so that even a German cannot tell you how it is bounded at any moment. The nation itself, with all its so-called internal improvements, which, by the way are all external and superficial, is just such an unwieldy and overgrown establishment, cluttered with furniture and tripped up by its own traps, ruined by luxury and heedless expense, by want of calculation and a worthy aim, as the million households in the land; and the only cure for it, as for them, is in a rigid economy, a stern and more than Spartan simplicity of life and elevation of purpose. It lives too fast. Men think that it is essential that the Nation have commerce, and export ice, and talk through a telegraph, and ride thirty miles an hour, without a doubt, whether they do or not; but whether we should live like baboons or like men, is a little uncertain. If we do not get out sleepers, and forge rails, and devote days and nights to the work, but go to tinkering upon our lives to improve them, who will build railroads? And if railroads are not built, how shall we get to heaven in season? But if we stay at home and mind our business, who will want railroads? We do not ride on the railroad; it rides upon us. Did you ever think what those sleepers are that underlie the railroad? Each one is a man, an Irishman, or a Yankee man. The rails are laid on them, and they are covered with sand, and the cars run smoothly over them. They are sound sleepers, I assure you. And every few years a new lot is laid down and run over; so that, if some have the pleasure of riding on a rail, others have the misfortune to be ridden upon. And when they run over a man that is walking in his sleep, a supernumerary sleeper in the wrong position, and wake him up, they suddenly stop the cars, and make a hue and cry about it, as if this were an exception. I am glad to know that it takes a gang of men for every five miles to keep the sleepers down and level in their beds as it is, for this is a sign that they may sometime get up again.

Why should we live with such hurry and waste of life? We are determined to be starved before we are hungry. Men say that a stitch in time saves nine, and so they take a thousand stitches today to save nine tomorrow. As for work, we haven't any of any consequence. We have the Saint Vitus' dance and cannot possibly keep our heads still. If I should only give a few pulls at the parish bell-rope, as for a fire, that is, without setting the bell, there is hardly a man on his farm in the outskirts of Concord, notwithstanding that press of engagements which was his excuse so many times this morning, nor a boy, nor a woman, I might almost say, but would forsake all and follow that sound, not mainly to save property from the flames, but, if we will confess the truth, much more to see it burn, since burn it must, and we, be it known, did not set it on fire -- or to see it put out, and have a hand in it, if that is done as handsomely; yes, even if it were the parish church itself. Hardly a man takes a half-hour's nap after dinner, but when he wakes he holds up his head and asks, "What's the news?" as if the rest of mankind had stood his sentinels. Some give directions to be waked every half-hour, doubtless for no other purpose; and then, to pay for it, they tell what they have dreamed. After a night's sleep the news is as indispensable as the breakfast. "Pray tell me anything new that has happened to a man anywhere on this globe" — and he reads it over his coffee and rolls, that a man has had his eyes gouged out this morning on the Wachito River; never dreaming the while that he lives in the dark unfathomed mammoth cave of this world and has but the rudiment of an eye himself.

For my part, I could easily do without the post-office. I think that there are very few important communications made through it. To speak critically, I never received more than one or two letters in my life — I wrote this some years ago — that were worth the postage. The penny-post is, commonly, an institution through which you seriously offer a man that penny for his thoughts which is so often safely offered in jest. And I am sure that I never read any memorable news in a newspaper. If we read of one man robbed, or murdered, or killed by accident, or one house burned, or one vessel wrecked, or one steamboat blown up, or one cow run over on the Western Railroad, or one mad dog killed, or one lot of grasshoppers in the winter -- we never need read of another. One is enough. If you are acquainted with the principle, what do you care for a myriad instances and applications? To a philosopher all news, as it is called, is gossip, and they who edit and read it are old women over their tea. Yet not a few are greedy after this gossip. There was such a rush, as I hear, the other day at one of the offices to learn the foreign news by the last arrival, that several large squares of plate glass belonging to the establishment were broken by the pressure — news which I seriously think a ready wit might write a twelve-month, or twelve years, beforehand with sufficient accuracy. As for Spain, for instance, if you know how to throw in Don Carlos and the Infanta, and Don Pedro and Seville and Granada, from time to time in the right proportions—they may have changed the names a little since I saw the papers—and serve up a bull-fight when other entertainments fail, it will be true to the letter, and give us as good an idea of the exact state or ruin of things in Spain as the most succinct and lucid reports under this head in the newspapers: and as for England, almost the last significant scrap of news from that quarter was the revolution of 1649; and if you have learned the history of her crops for an average year, you never need attend to that thing again, unless your speculations are of a merely pecuniary character. If one may judge who rarely looks into the newspapers, nothing new does ever happen in foreign parts, a French revolution not excepted.

What news! how much more important to know what that is which was never old! "Kieou-he-yu (great dignitary of the state of Wei) sent a man to Khoung-tseu to know his news. Khoung-tseu caused the messenger to be seated near him, and questioned him in these terms: What is your master doing? The messenger answered with respect: My master desires to diminish the number of his faults, but he cannot come to the end of them. The messenger being gone, the philosopher remarked: What a worthy messenger! What a worthy messenger!" The preacher, instead of vexing the ears of drowsy farmers on their day of rest at the end of the week — for Sunday is the fit conclusion of an ill-spent week, and not the fresh and brave beginning of a new one — with this one other draggle-tail of a sermon, should shout with thundering voice, "Pause! Avast! Why so seeming fast, but deadly slow?"

Shams and delusions are esteemed for soundest truths, while reality is fabulous. If men would steadily observe realities only, and not allow themselves to be deluded, life, to compare it with such things as we know, would be like a fairy tale and the Arabian Nights' Entertainments. If we respected only what is inevitable and has a right to be, music and poetry would resound along the streets. When we are unhurried and wise, we perceive that only great and worthy things have any permanent and absolute existence, that petty fears and petty pleasures are but the shadow of the reality. This is always exhilarating and sublime. By closing the eyes and slumbering, and consenting to be deceived by shows, men establish and confirm their daily life of routine and habit everywhere, which still is built on purely illusory foundations. Children, who play life, discern its true law and relations more clearly than men, who fail to live it worthily, but who think that they are wiser by experience, that is, by failure. I have read in a Hindoo book, that "there was a king's son, who, being expelled in infancy from his native city, was brought up by a forester, and, growing up to maturity in that state, imagined himself to belong to the barbarous race with which he lived. One of his father's ministers having discovered him, revealed to him what he was, and the misconception of his character was removed, and he knew himself to be a prince. So soul," continues the Hindoo philosopher, "from the circumstances in which it is placed, mistakes its own character, until the truth is revealed to it by some holy teacher, and then it knows itself to be *Brahme*." I perceive that we inhabitants of New England live this mean life that we do because our vision does not penetrate the surface of things. We think that that is which *appears* to be. If a man should walk through this town and see only the reality, where, think you, would the "Mill-dam" go to? If he should give us an account of the realities he beheld there, we should not recognize the place in his description. Look at a meeting-house, or a courthouse, or a jail, or a shop, or a dwelling-house, and say what that thing really is before a true gaze, and they would all go to pieces in your account of them. Men esteem truth remote, in the outskirts of the system, behind the farthest star, before Adam and after the last man. In eternity there is indeed something true and sublime. But all these times and places and occasions are now and here. God himself culminates in the present moment and will never be more divine in the lapse of all the ages. And we are enabled to apprehend at all what is sublime and noble only by the perpetual instilling and drenching of the reality that surrounds us. The universe constantly and obediently answers to our conceptions; whether we travel fast or slow, the track is laid for us. Let us spend our lives in conceiving then. The poet or the artist never yet had so fair and noble a design but some of his posterity at least could accomplish it.

Let us spend one day as deliberately as Nature and not be thrown off the track by every nutshell and mosquito's wing that falls on the rails. Let us rise early and fast, or break fast, gently and without perturbation; let company come and let company go, let the bells ring and the children cry — determined to make a day of it. Why should we knock under and go with the stream? Let us not be upset and overwhelmed in that terrible rapid and whirlpool called a dinner, situated in the meridian shallows. Weather this danger and you are safe, for the rest of the way is downhill. With unrelaxed nerves, with morning vigor, sail by it, looking another way, tied to the mast like Ulysses. If the engine whistles, let it whistle till it is hoarse for its pains. If the bell rings, why should we run? We will consider what kind of music they are like. Let us settle ourselves, and work and wedge our feet downward through the mud and slush of opinion, and prejudice, and tradition, and delusion, and appearance, that alluvion which covers the globe, through Paris and London, through New York and Boston and Concord, through Church and State, through poetry and philosophy and religion, till we come to a hard bottom and rocks in place, which we can call *reality*, and say, This is, and no mistake; and then begin, having a *point d'appui*, below freshet and frost and fire, a place where you might found a wall or a state, or set a lamp-post safely, or perhaps a gauge, not a Nilometer, but a Realometer, that future ages might know how deep a freshet of shams and appearances had gathered from time to time. If you stand right fronting and face to face to a fact, you will see the sun glimmer on both its surfaces, as if it were a cimeter, and feel its sweet edge dividing you through the heart and marrow, and so you will happily conclude your mortal career. Be it life or death, we crave only reality. If we are really dying, let us hear the rattle in our throats and feel cold in the extremities; if we are alive, let us go about our business.

Time is but the stream I go a-fishing in. I drink at it; but while I drink, I see the sandy bottom and detect how shallow it is. Its thin current slides away, but eternity remains. I would drink deeper; fish in the sky, whose bottom is pebbly with stars. I cannot count one. I know not the first letter of the alphabet. I have always been regretting that I was not as wise as the day I was born. The intellect is a cleaver; it discerns and rifts its way into the secret of things. I do not wish to be any more busy with my hands than is necessary. My head is hands and feet. I feel all my best faculties concentrated in it. My instinct tells me that my head is an organ for burrowing, as some creatures use their snout and fore paws, and with it I would mine and burrow my way through these hills. I think that the richest vein is somewhere hereabouts; so by the divining-rod and thin rising vapors I judge; and here I will begin to mine.

XV
Winter Animals

When the ponds were firmly frozen, they afforded not only new and shorter routes to many points, but new views from their surfaces of the familiar landscape around them. When I crossed Flint's Pond, after it was covered with snow, though I had often paddled about and skated over it, it was so unexpectedly wide and so strange that I could think of nothing but Baffin's Bay. The Lincoln hills rose up around me at the extremity of a snowy plain, in which I did not remember to have stood before; and the fishermen, at an indeterminable distance over the ice, moving slowly about with their wolfish dogs, passed for sealers, or Esquimaux, or in misty weather loomed like fabulous creatures, and I did not know whether they were giants or pygmies. I took this course when I went to lecture in Lincoln in the evening, travelling in no road and passing no house between my own hut and the lecture room. In Goose Pond, which lay in my way, a colony of muskrats dwelt, and raised their cabins high above the ice, though none could be seen abroad when I crossed it. Walden, being like the rest usually bare of snow, or with only shallow and interrupted drifts on it, was my yard where I could walk freely when the snow was nearly two feet deep on a level elsewhere and the villagers were confined to their streets. There, far from the village street, and except at very long intervals, from the jingle of sleighbells, I slid and skated, as in a vast moose–yard well-trodden, overhung by oak woods and solemn pines bent down with snow or bristling with icicles.

For sounds in winter nights, and often in winter days, I heard the forlorn but melodious note of a hooting owl indefinitely far; such a sound as the frozen earth would yield if struck with a suitable plectrum, the very *lingua vernacula* of Walden Wood, and quite familiar to me at last, though I never saw the bird while it was making it. I seldom opened my door in a winter evening without hearing it; *Hoo hoo hoo, hoorer, hoo*, sounded sonorously, and the first three syllables accented somewhat like *how der do*; or sometimes *hoo, hoo* only. One night in the beginning of winter, before the pond froze over, about nine o'clock, I was startled by the loud honking of a goose, and, stepping to the door, heard the sound of their wings like a tempest in the woods as they flew low over my house. They passed over the pond toward Fair Haven, seemingly deterred from settling by my light, their commodore honking all the while with a regular beat. Suddenly an unmistakable cat–owl from very near me, with the most harsh and tremendous voice I ever heard from any inhabitant of the woods, responded at regular intervals to the goose, as if determined to expose and disgrace this intruder from Hudson's Bay by exhibiting a greater compass and volume of voice in a native, and *boo–hoo* him out of Concord horizon. What do you mean by alarming the citadel at this time of night consecrated to me? Do you think I am ever caught napping at such an hour, and that I have not got lungs and a larynx as well as yourself? *Boo–hoo, boo–hoo, boo–hoo*! It was one of the most thrilling discords I ever heard. And yet, if you had a discriminating ear, there were in it the elements of a concord such as these plains never saw nor heard.

I also heard the whooping of the ice in the pond, my great bed–fellow in that part of Concord, as if it were restless in its bed and would fain turn over, were troubled with flatulency and had dreams; or I was waked by the cracking of the ground by the frost, as if someone had driven a team against my door, and in the morning would find a crack in the earth a quarter of a mile long and a third of an inch wide.

Sometimes I heard the foxes as they ranged over the snow–crust, in moonlight nights, in search of a partridge or other game, barking raggedly and demoniacally like forest dogs, as if laboring with some anxiety, or seeking expression, struggling for light and to be dogs outright and run freely in the streets; for if we take the ages into our account, may there not be a civilization going on among brutes as well as men? They seemed to me to be rudimental, burrowing men, still standing on their defence, awaiting their transformation. Sometimes one came near to my window, attracted by my light, barked a vulpine curse at me, and then retreated.

Usually the red squirrel (*Sciurus Hudsonius*) waked me in the dawn, coursing over the roof and up and down the sides of the house, as if sent out of the woods for this purpose. In the course of the winter I threw out half a bushel of ears of sweet corn, which had not got ripe, on to the snow–crust by my door, and was amused by watching the motions of the various animals which were baited by it. In the twilight and the night the rabbits came regularly and made a hearty meal. All day long the red squirrels came and went, and afforded me much entertainment by their manoeuvres. One would approach at first warily through the shrub oaks, running over the snow–crust by fits and starts like a leaf blown by the wind, now a few paces this way, with wonderful speed and waste of energy, making inconceivable haste with his "trotters," as if it were for a wager, and now as many paces that way, but never getting on more than half a rod at a time; and then suddenly pausing with a ludicrous expression and a gratuitous somerset, as if all the eyes in the universe were eyed on him—for all the motions of a squirrel, even in the most solitary recesses of the forest, imply spectators as much as those of a dancing girl—wasting more time in delay and circumspection than would have sufficed to walk the whole distance—I never saw one walk—and then suddenly, before you could say Jack Robinson, he would be in the top of a young pitch pine, winding up his clock and chiding all imaginary spectators, soliloquizing and talking to all the universe at the same time—for no reason that I could ever detect, or he himself was aware of, I suspect. At length he would reach the corn, and selecting a suitable ear, frisk about in the same uncertain trigonometrical way to the topmost stick of my wood–pile, before my window, where he looked me in the face, and there sit for hours, supplying himself with a new ear from time to time, nibbling at first voraciously and throwing the half–naked cobs about; till at length he grew more dainty still and played with his food, tasting only the inside of the kernel, and the ear, which was held balanced over the stick by one paw, slipped from his careless grasp and fell to the ground, when he would look over at it with a ludicrous expression of uncertainty, as if suspecting that it had life, with a mind not made up whether to get it again, or a new one, or be off; now thinking of corn, then listening to hear what was in the wind. So the little impudent fellow would waste many an ear in a forenoon; till at last, seizing some longer and plumper one, considerably bigger than himself, and skillfully balancing it, he would set out with it to the woods, like a tiger with a buffalo, by the same zig–zag course and frequent pauses, scratching along with it as if it were too heavy for him and falling all the while, making its fall a diagonal between a perpendicular and horizontal, being determined to put it through at any rate;—a singularly frivolous and whimsical fellow;—and so he would get off with it to where he lived, perhaps carry it to the top of a pine tree forty or fifty rods distant, and I would afterwards find the cobs strewn about the woods in various directions.

At length the jays arrive, whose discordant screams were heard long before, as they were warily making their approach an eighth of a mile off, and in a stealthy and sneaking manner they flit from tree to tree, nearer and nearer, and pick up the kernels which the squirrels have dropped. Then, sitting on a pitch pine bough, they attempt to swallow in their haste a kernel which is too big for their throats and chokes them; and after great labor they disgorge it, and spend an hour in the endeavor to crack it by repeated blows with their bills. They were manifestly thieves, and I had not much respect for them; but the squirrels, though at first shy, went to work as if they were taking what was their own.

Meanwhile also came the chickadees in flocks, which, picking up the crumbs the squirrels had dropped, flew to the nearest twig and placing them under their claws, hammered away at them with their little bills, as if it were an insect in the bark, till they were sufficiently reduced for their slender throats. A little flock of these titmice came daily to pick a dinner out of my woodpile, or the crumbs at my door, with faint flitting lisping notes, like the tinkling of icicles in the grass, or else with sprightly *day day day*, or more rarely, in spring–like days, a wiry summery *phe–be* from the woodside. They were so familiar that at length one alighted on an armful of wood which I was carrying in and pecked at the sticks without fear. I once had a sparrow alight upon my shoulder for a moment while I was hoeing in a village garden, and I felt that I was more distinguished by that circumstance than I should have been by any epaulet I could have worn. The squirrels also grew at last to be quite familiar, and occasionally stepped upon my shoe, when that was the nearest way.

When the ground was not yet quite covered, and again near the end of winter, when the snow was melted on my south hillside and about my woodpile, the partridges came out of the woods morning and evening to feed there. Whichever side you walk in the woods the partridge bursts away on whirring wings, jarring the snow from the dry leaves and twigs on high, which comes sifting down in the sunbeams like golden dust, for this brave bird is not to be scared by winter. It is frequently covered up by drifts, and, it is said, "sometimes plunges from on wing into the soft snow, where it remains concealed for a day or two." I used to start them in the open land also, where they had come out of the woods at sunset to "bud" the wild apple trees. They will come regularly every evening to particular trees, where the cunning sportsman lies in wait for them, and the distant orchards next the woods suffer thus not a little. I am glad that the partridge gets fed, at any rate. It is Nature's own bird which lives on buds and diet drink.

In dark winter mornings, or in short winter afternoons, I sometimes heard a pack of hounds threading all the woods with hounding cry and yelp, unable to resist the instinct of the chase, and the note of the hunting–horn at intervals, proving that man was in the rear. The woods ring again, and yet no fox bursts forth on to the open level of the pond, nor following pack pursuing their Actaeon. And perhaps at evening I see the hunters returning with a single brush trailing from their sleigh for a trophy, seeking their inn. They tell me that if the fox would remain in the bosom of the frozen earth he would be safe, or if he would run in a straight line away no foxhound could overtake him; but, having left his pursuers far behind, he stops to rest and listen till they come up, and when he runs he circles round to his old haunts, where the hunters await him. Sometimes, however, he will run upon a wall many rods, and then leap off far to one side, and he appears to know that water will not retain his scent. A hunter told me that he once saw a fox pursued by hounds burst out on to Walden when the ice was covered with shallow puddles, run part way across, and then return to the same shore. Ere long the hounds arrived, but here they lost the scent. Sometimes a pack hunting by themselves would pass my door, and circle round my house, and yelp and hound without regarding me, as if afflicted by a species of madness, so that nothing could divert them from the pursuit. Thus they circle until they fall upon the recent trail of a fox, for a wise hound will forsake everything else for this. One day a man came to my hut from Lexington to inquire after his hound that made a large track, and had been hunting for a week by himself. But I fear that he was not the wiser for all I told him, for every time I attempted to answer his questions he interrupted me by asking, "What do you do here?" He had lost a dog but found a man.

One old hunter who has a dry tongue, who used to come to bathe in Walden once every year when the water was warmest, and at such times looked in upon me, told me that many years ago he took his gun one afternoon and went out for a cruise in Walden Wood; and as he walked the Wayland road he heard the cry of hounds approaching, and ere long a fox leaped the wall into the road, and as quick as thought leaped the other wall out of the road, and his swift bullet had not touched him. Some way behind came an old hound and her three pups in full pursuit, hunting on their own account, and disappeared again in the woods. Late in the afternoon, as he was resting in the thick woods south of Walden, he heard the voice of the hounds far over toward Fair Haven still pursuing the fox; and on they came, their hounding cry which made all the woods ring sounding nearer and nearer, now from Well Meadow, now from the Baker Farm. For a long time he stood still and listened to their music, so sweet to a hunter's ear, when suddenly the fox appeared, threading the solemn aisles with an easy coursing pace, whose sound was concealed by a sympathetic rustle of the leaves, swift and still, keeping the round, leaving his pursuers far behind; and, leaping upon a rock amid the woods, he sat erect and listening, with his back to the hunter. For a moment compassion restrained the latter's arm; but that was a short–lived mood, and as quick as thought can follow thought his piece was levelled, and whang! The fox, rolling over the rock, lay dead on the ground. The hunter still kept his place and listened to the hounds. Still on they came, and now the near woods resounded through all their aisles with their demoniac cry. At length the old hound burst into view with muzzle to the ground, and snapping the air as if possessed, and ran directly to the rock; but, spying the dead fox, she suddenly ceased her hounding as if struck dumb with amazement, and walked round and round him in silence; and one by one her pups arrived, and, like their mother, were sobered into silence by the mystery. Then the hunter came forward and stood in their midst, and the mystery was solved. They waited in silence while he skinned the fox, then followed the brush a while, and at length turned off into the woods again. That evening a Weston squire came to the Concord hunter's cottage to inquire for his hounds, and told how for a week they had been hunting on their own account from Weston woods. The Concord hunter told him what he knew and offered him the skin; but the other declined it and departed. He did not find his hounds that night, but the next day learned that they had crossed the river and put up at a farmhouse for the night, whence, having been well fed, they took their departure early in the morning.

The hunter who told me this could remember one Sam Nutting, who used to hunt bears on Fair Haven Ledges, and exchange their skins for rum in Concord village; who told him, even, that he had seen a moose there. Nutting had a famous foxhound named Burgoyne—he pronounced it Bugine—which my informant used to borrow. In the "Wast Book" of an old trader of this town, who was also a captain, town–clerk, and representative, I find the following entry. Jan. 18th, 1742–3, "John Melven Cr. by 1 Grey Fox 0—2—3"; they are not now found here; and in his ledger, Feb, 7th, 1743, Hezekiah Stratton has credit "by 1/2 a Catt skin 0—1—4+"; of course, a wild–cat, for Stratton was a sergeant in the old French war, and would not have got credit for hunting less noble game. Credit is given for deerskins also, and they were daily sold. One man still preserves the horns of the last deer that was killed in this vicinity, and another has told me the particulars of the hunt in which his uncle was engaged. The hunters were formerly a numerous and merry crew here. I remember well one gaunt Nimrod who would catch up a leaf by the roadside and play a strain on it wilder and more melodious, if my memory serves me, than any hunting–horn.

At midnight, when there was a moon, I sometimes met with hounds in my path prowling about the woods, which would skulk out of my way, as if afraid, and stand silent amid the bushes till I had passed.

Squirrels and wild mice disputed for my store of nuts. There were scores of pitch pines around my house, from one to four inches in diameter, which had been gnawed by mice the previous winter—a Norwegian winter for them, for the snow lay long and deep, and they were obliged to mix a large proportion of pine bark with their other diet. These trees were alive and apparently flourishing at midsummer, and many of them had grown a foot, though completely girdled; but after another winter such were without exception dead. It is remarkable that a single mouse should thus be allowed a whole pine tree for its dinner, gnawing round instead of up and down it; but perhaps it is necessary in order to thin these trees, which are wont to grow up densely.

The hares (*Lepus Americanus*) were very familiar. One had her form under my house all winter, separated from me only by the flooring, and she startled me each morning by her hasty departure when I began to stir—thump, thump, thump, striking her head against the floor timbers in her hurry. They used to come round my door at dusk to nibble the potato parings which I had thrown out and were so nearly the color of the ground that they could hardly be distinguished when still. Sometimes in the twilight I alternately lost and recovered sight of one sitting motionless under my window. When I opened my door in the evening, off they would go with a squeak and a bounce. Near at hand they only excited my pity. One evening one sat by my door two paces from me, at first trembling with fear, yet unwilling to move; a poor wee thing, lean and bony, with ragged ears and sharp nose, scant tail and slender paws. It looked as if Nature no longer contained the breed of nobler bloods, but stood on her last toes. Its large eyes appeared young and unhealthy, almost dropsical. I took a step, and lo, away it scud with an elastic spring over the snow–crust, straightening its body and its limbs into graceful length, and soon put the forest between me and itself—the wild free venison, asserting its vigor and the dignity of Nature. Not without reason was its slenderness. Such then was its nature. (*Lepus, levipes*, light–foot, some think.)

What is a country without rabbits and partridges? They are among the most simple and indigenous animal products; ancient and venerable families known to antiquity as to modern times; of the very hue and substance of Nature, nearest allied to leaves and to the ground—and to one another; it is either winged or it is legged. It is hardly as if you had seen a wild creature when a rabbit or a partridge bursts away, only a natural one, as much to be expected as rustling leaves. The partridge and the rabbit are still sure to thrive, like true natives of the soil, whatever revolutions occur. If the forest is cut off, the sprouts and bushes which spring up afford them concealment, and they become more numerous than ever. That must be a poor country indeed that does not support a hare. Our woods teem with them both, and around every swamp may be seen the partridge or rabbit walk, beset with twiggy fences and horse–hair snares, which some cow–boy tends.

XVI
The Pond in Winter

After a still winter night I awoke with the impression that some question had been put to me, which I had been endeavoring in vain to answer in my sleep, as what—how—when—where? But there was dawning Nature, in whom all creatures live, looking in at my broad windows with serene and satisfied face, and no question on *her* lips. I awoke to an answered question, to Nature and daylight. The snow lying deep on the earth dotted with young pines, and the very slope of the hill on which my house is placed, seemed to say, Forward! Nature puts no question and answers none which we mortals ask. She has long ago taken her resolution. "O Prince, our eyes contemplate with admiration and transmit to the soul the wonderful and varied spectacle of this universe. The night veils without doubt a part of this glorious creation; but day comes to reveal to us this great work, which extends from earth even into the plains of the ether."

Then to my morning work. First I take an axe and pail and go in search of water, if that be not a dream. After a cold and snowy night it needed a divining rod to find it. Every winter the liquid and trembling surface of the pond, which was so sensitive to every breath, and reflected every light and shadow, becomes solid to the depth of a foot or a foot and a half, so that it will support the heaviest teams, and perchance the snow covers it to an equal depth, and it is not to be distinguished from any level field. Like the marmots in the surrounding hills, it closes its eye-lids and becomes dormant for three months or more. Standing on the snow-covered plain, as if in a pasture amid the hills, I cut my way first through a foot of snow, and then a foot of ice, and open a window under my feet, where, kneeling to drink, I look down into the quiet parlor of the fishes, pervaded by a softened light as through a window of ground glass, with its bright sanded floor the same as in summer; there a perennial waveless serenity reigns as in the amber twilight sky, corresponding to the cool and even temperament of the inhabitants. Heaven is under our feet as well as over our heads.

Early in the morning, while all things are crisp with frost, men come with fishing reels and slender lunch, and let down their fine lines through the snowy field to take pickerel and perch; wild men, who instinctively follow other fashions and trust other authorities than their townsmen, and by their goings and comings stitch towns together in parts where else they would be ripped. They sit and eat their luncheon in stout fear-naughts on the dry oak leaves on the shore, as wise in natural lore as the citizen is in artificial. They never consulted with books and know and can tell much less than they have done. The things which they practise are said not yet to be known. Here is one fishing for pickerel with grown perch for bait. You look into his pail with wonder as into a summer pond, as if he kept summer locked up at home, or knew where she had retreated. How, pray, did he get these in mid-winter? O, he got worms out of rotten logs since the ground froze, and so he caught them. His life itself passes deeper in Nature than the studies of the naturalist penetrate; himself a subject for the naturalist. The latter raises the moss and bark gently with his knife in search of insects; the former lays open logs to their core with his axe, and moss and bark fly far and wide. He gets his living by barking trees. Such a man has some right to fish, and I love to see Nature carried out in him. The perch swallows the grub-worm, the pickerel swallows the perch, and the fisherman swallows the pickerel; and so all the chinks in the scale of being are filled.

When I strolled around the pond in misty weather I was sometimes amused by the primitive mode which some ruder fisherman had adopted. He would perhaps have placed alder branches over the narrow holes in the ice, which were four or five rods apart and an equal distance from the shore, and having fastened the end of the line to a stick to prevent its being pulled through, have passed the slack line over a twig of the alder, a foot or more above the ice, and tied a dry oak leaf to it, which, being pulled down, would show when he had a bite. These alders loomed through the mist at regular intervals as you walked halfway round the pond.

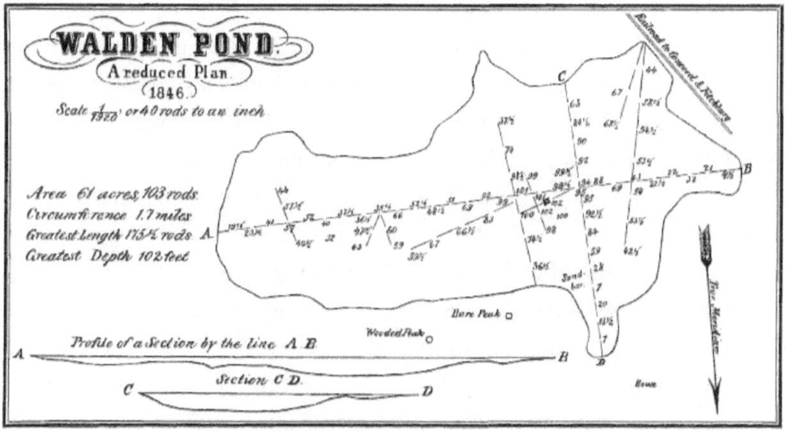

Ah, the pickerel of Walden! when I see them lying on the ice, or in the well which the fisherman cuts in the ice, making a little hole to admit the water, I am always surprised by their rare beauty, as if they were fabulous fishes, they are so foreign to the streets, even to the woods, foreign as Arabia to our Concord life. They possess a quite dazzling and transcendent beauty which separates them by a wide interval from the cadaverous cod and haddock whose fame is trumpeted in our streets. They are not green like the pines, nor gray like the stones, nor blue like the sky; but they have, to my eyes, if possible, yet rarer colors, like flowers and precious stones, as if they were the pearls, the animalized *nuclei* or crystals of the Walden water. They, of course, are Walden all over and all through; are themselves small Waldens in the animal kingdom, Waldenses. It is surprising that they are caught here,—that in this deep and capacious spring, far beneath the rattling teams and chaises and tinkling sleighs that travel the Walden road, this great gold and emerald fish swims. I never chanced to see its kind in any market; it would be the cynosure of all eyes there. Easily, with a few convulsive quirks, they give up their watery ghosts, like a mortal translated before his time to the thin air of heaven.

As I was desirous to recover the long-lost bottom of Walden Pond, I surveyed it carefully, before the ice broke up, early in '46, with compass and chain and sounding line. There have been many stories told about the bottom, or rather no bottom, of this pond, which certainly had no foundation for themselves. It is remarkable how long men will believe in the bottomlessness of a pond without taking the trouble to sound it. I have visited two such Bottomless Ponds in one walk in this neighborhood. Many have believed that Walden reached quite through to the other side of the globe. Some who have lain flat on the ice for a long time, looking down through the illusive medium, perchance with watery eyes into the bargain, and driven to hasty conclusions by the fear of catching cold in their breasts, have seen vast holes "into which a load of hay might be driven," if there were any body to drive it, the undoubted source of the Styx and entrance to the Infernal Regions from these parts. Others have gone down from the village with a "fifty-six" and a wagon load of inch rope but yet have failed to find any bottom; for while the "fifty-six" was resting by the way, they were paying out the rope in the vain attempt to fathom their truly immeasurable capacity for marvellousness. But I can assure my readers that Walden has a reasonably tight bottom at a not unreasonable, though at an unusual, depth. I fathomed it easily with a cod-line and a stone weighing about a pound and a half and could tell accurately when the stone left the bottom, by having to pull so much harder before the water got underneath to help me. The greatest depth was exactly one hundred and two feet; to which may be added the five feet which it has risen since, making one hundred and seven. This is a remarkable depth for so small an area; yet not an inch of it can be spared by the imagination. What if all ponds were shallow? Would it not react on the minds of men? I am thankful that this pond was made deep and pure for a symbol. While men believe in the infinite some ponds will be thought to be bottomless.

A factory owner, hearing what depth I had found, thought that it could not be true, for, judging from his acquaintance with dams, sand would not lie at so steep an angle. But the deepest ponds are not so deep in proportion to their area as most suppose, and, if drained, would not leave very remarkable valleys. They are not like cups between the hills; for this one, which is so unusually deep for its area, appears in a vertical section through its centre not deeper than a shallow plate. Most ponds, emptied, would leave a meadow no more hollow than we frequently see. William Gilpin, who is so admirable in all that relates to landscapes, and usually so correct, standing at the head of Loch Fyne, in Scotland, which he describes as "a bay of salt water, sixty or seventy fathoms deep, four miles in breadth," and about fifty miles long, surrounded by mountains, observes, "If we could have seen it immediately after the diluvian crash, or whatever convulsion of Nature occasioned it, before the waters gushed in, what a horrid chasm must it have appeared!

> So high as heaved the tumid hills, so low
> Down sunk a hollow bottom broad and deep,
> Capacious bed of waters—"

But if, using the shortest diameter of Loch Fyne, we apply these proportions to Walden, which, as we have seen, appears already in a vertical section only like a shallow plate, it will appear four times as shallow. So much for the *increased* horrors of the chasm of Loch Fyne when emptied. No doubt many a smiling valley with its stretching cornfields occupies exactly such a "horrid chasm," from which the waters have receded, though it requires the insight and the far sight of the geologist to convince the unsuspecting inhabitants of this fact. Often an inquisitive eye may detect the shores of a primitive lake in the low horizon hills, and no subsequent elevation of the plain has been necessary to conceal their history. But it is easiest, as they who work on the highways know, to find the hollows by the puddles after a shower. The amount of it is, the imagination give it the least license, dives deeper and soars higher than Nature goes. So, probably, the depth of the ocean will be found to be very inconsiderable compared with its breadth.

As I sounded through the ice I could determine the shape of the bottom with greater accuracy than is possible in surveying harbors which do not freeze over, and I was surprised at its general regularity. In the deepest part there are several acres more level than almost any field which is exposed to the sun wind and plough. In one instance, on a line arbitrarily chosen, the depth did not vary more than one foot in thirty rods; and generally, near the middle, I could calculate the variation for each one hundred feet in any direction beforehand within three or four inches. Some are accustomed to speak of deep and dangerous holes even in quiet sandy ponds like this, but the effect of water under these circumstances is to level all inequalities. The regularity of the bottom and its conformity to the shores and the range of the neighboring hills were so perfect that a distant promontory betrayed itself in the soundings quite across the pond, and its direction could be determined by observing the opposite shore. Cape becomes bar, and plain shoal, and valley and gorge deep water and channel.

When I had mapped the pond by the scale of ten rods to an inch, and put down the soundings, more than a hundred in all, I observed this remarkable coincidence. Having noticed that the number indicating the greatest depth was apparently in the centre of the map, I laid a rule on the map lengthwise, and then breadthwise, and found, to my surprise, that the line of greatest length intersected the line of greatest breadth *exactly* at the point of greatest depth, notwithstanding that the middle is so nearly level, the outline of the pond far from regular, and the extreme length and breadth were got by measuring into the coves; and I said to myself, Who knows but this hint would conduct to the deepest part of the ocean as well as of a pond or puddle? Is not this the rule also for the height of mountains, regarded as the opposite of valleys? We know that a hill is not highest at its narrowest part.

Of five coves, three, or all which had been sounded, were observed to have a bar quite across their mouths and deeper water within, so that the bay tended to be an expansion of water within the land not only horizontally but vertically, and to form a basin or independent pond, the direction of the two capes showing the course of the bar. Every harbor on the sea-coast, also, has its bar at its entrance. In proportion as the mouth of the cove was wider compared with its length, the water over the bar was deeper compared with that in the basin. Given, then, the length and breadth of the cove, and the character of the surrounding shore, and you have almost elements enough to make out a formula for all cases.

In order to see how nearly I could guess, with this experience, at the deepest point in a pond, by observing the outlines of its surface and the character of its shores alone, I made a plan of White Pond, which contains about forty-one acres, and, like this, has no island in it, nor any visible inlet or outlet; and as the line of greatest breadth fell very near the line of least breadth, where two opposite capes approached each other and two opposite bays receded, I ventured to mark a point a short distance from the latter line, but still on the line of greatest length, as the deepest. The deepest part was found to be within one hundred feet of this, still farther in the direction to which I had inclined, and was only one foot deeper, namely, sixty feet. Of course, a stream running through, or an island in the pond, would make the problem much more complicated.

If we knew all the laws of Nature, we should need only one fact, or the description of one actual phenomenon, to infer all the particular results at that point. Now we know only a few laws, and our result is vitiated, not, of course, by any confusion or irregularity in Nature, but by our ignorance of essential elements in the calculation. Our notions of law and harmony are commonly confined to those instances which we detect; but the harmony which results from a far greater number of seemingly conflicting, but really concurring, laws, which we have not detected, is still more wonderful. The particular laws are as our points of view, as, to the traveller, a mountain outline varies with every step, and it has an infinite number of profiles, though absolutely but one form. Even when cleft or bored through it is not comprehended in its entireness.

What I have observed of the pond is no less true in ethics. It is the law of average. Such a rule of the two diameters not only guides us toward the sun in the system and the heart in man but draw lines through the length and breadth of the aggregate of a man's particular daily behaviors and waves of life into his coves and inlets, and where they intersect will be the height or depth of his character. Perhaps we need only to know how his shores trend and his adjacent country or circumstances, to infer his depth and concealed bottom. If he is surrounded by mountainous circumstances, an Achillean shore, whose peaks overshadow and are reflected in his bosom, they suggest a corresponding depth in him. But a low and smooth shore proves him shallow on that side. In our bodies, a bold projecting brow falls off to and indicates a corresponding depth of thought. Also there is a bar across the entrance of our every cove, or particular inclination; each is our harbor for a season, in which we are detained and partially land locked. These inclinations are not whimsical usually, but their form, size, and direction are determined by the promontories of the shore, the ancient axes of elevation. When this bar is gradually increased by storms, tides, or currents, or there is a subsidence of the waters, so that it reaches to the surface, that which was at first but an inclination in the shore in which a thought was harbored becomes an individual lake, cut off from the ocean, wherein the thought secures its own conditions, changes, perhaps, from salt to fresh, becomes a sweet sea, dead sea, or a marsh. At the advent of each individual into this life, may we not suppose that such a bar has risen to the surface somewhere? It is true, we are such poor navigators that our thoughts, for the most part, stand off and on upon a harborless coast, are conversant only with the bights of the bays of poesy, or steer for the public ports of entry, and go into the dry docks of science, where they merely refit for this world, and no natural currents concur to individualize them.

As for the inlet or outlet of Walden, I have not discovered any but rain and snow and evaporation, though perhaps, with a thermometer and a line, such places may be found, for where the water flows into the pond it will probably be coldest in summer and warmest in winter. When the ice-men were at work here in '46–7, the cakes sent to the shore were one day rejected by those who were stacking them up there, not being thick enough to lie side by side with the rest; and the cutters thus discovered that the ice over a small space was two or three inches thinner than elsewhere, which made them think that there was an inlet there. They also showed me in another place what they thought was a "leach hole," through which the pond leaked out under a hill into a neighboring meadow, pushing me out on a cake of ice to see it. It was a small cavity under ten feet of water; but I think that I can warrant the pond not to need soldering till they find a worse leak than that. One has suggested, that if such a "leach hole" should be found, its connection with the meadow, if any existed, might be proved by conveying some colored powder or sawdust to the mouth of the hole, and then putting a strainer over the spring in the meadow, which would catch some of the particles carried through by the current.

While I was surveying, the ice, which was sixteen inches thick, undulated under a slight wind like water. It is well known that a level cannot be used on ice. At one rod from the shore its greatest fluctuation, when observed by means of a level on land directed toward a graduated staff on the ice, was three quarters of an inch, though the ice appeared firmly attached to the shore. It was probably greater in the middle. Who knows but if our instruments were delicate enough we might detect an undulation in the crust of the earth? When two legs of my level were on the shore and the third on the ice, and the sights were directed over the latter, a rise or fall of the ice of an almost infinitesimal amount made a difference of several feet on a tree across the pond. When I began to cut holes for sounding, there were three or four inches of water on the ice under a deep snow which had sunk it thus far; but the water began immediately to run into these holes, and continued to run for two days in deep streams, which wore away the ice on every side, and contributed essentially, if not mainly, to dry the surface of the pond; for, as the water ran in, it raised and floated the ice. This was somewhat like cutting a hole in the bottom of a ship to let the water out. When such holes freeze, and a rain succeeds, and finally a new freezing forms a fresh smooth ice over all, it is beautifully mottled internally by dark figures, shaped somewhat like a spider's web, what you may call ice rosettes, produced by the channels worn by the water flowing from all sides to a centre. Sometimes, also, when the ice was covered with shallow puddles, I saw a double shadow of myself, one standing on the head of the other, one on the ice, the other on the trees or hill-side.

While yet it is cold January, and snow and ice are thick and solid, the prudent landlord comes from the village to get ice to cool his summer drink; impressively, even pathetically wise, to foresee the heat and thirst of July now in January, —wearing a thick coat and mittens! when so many things are not provided for. It may be that he lays up no treasures in this world which will cool his summer drink in the next. He cuts and saws the solid pond, unroofs the house of fishes, and carts off their very element and air, held fast by chains and stakes like corded wood, through the favoring winter air, to wintry cellars, to underlie the summer there. It looks like solidified azure, as, far off, it is drawn through the streets. These ice-cutters are a merry race, full of jest and sport, and when I went among them they were wont to invite me to saw pit-fashion with them, I standing underneath.

In the winter of '46–7 there came a hundred men of Hyperborean extraction swoop down on to our pond one morning, with many carloads of ungainly-looking farming tools, sleds, ploughs, drill-barrows, turf-knives, spades, saws, rakes, and each man was armed with a double-pointed pike-staff, such as is not described in the New-England Farmer or the Cultivator. I did not know whether they had come to sow a crop of winter rye, or some other kind of grain recently introduced from Iceland. As I saw no manure, I judged that they meant to skim the land, as I had done, thinking the soil was deep and had lain fallow long enough. They said that a gentleman farmer, who was behind the scenes, wanted to double his money, which, as I understood, amounted to half a million already; but in order to cover each one of his dollars with another, he took off the only coat, ay, the skin itself, of Walden Pond in the midst of a hard winter. They went to work at once, ploughing, harrowing, rolling, furrowing, in admirable order, as if they were bent on making this a model farm; but when I was looking sharp to see what kind of seed they dropped into the furrow, a gang of fellows by my side suddenly began to hook up the virgin mould itself, with a peculiar jerk, clean down to the sand, or rather the water,—for it was a very springy soil,—indeed all the *terra firma* there was,—and haul it away on sleds, and then I guessed that they must be cutting peat in a bog. So they came and went every day, with a peculiar shriek from the locomotive, from and to some point of the polar regions, as it seemed to me, like a flock of arctic snow-birds. But sometimes Squaw Walden had her revenge, and a hired man, walking behind his team, slipped through a crack in the ground down toward Tartarus, and he who was so brave before suddenly became but the ninth part of a man, almost gave up his animal heat, and was glad to take refuge in my house, and acknowledged that there was some virtue in a stove; or sometimes the frozen soil took a piece of steel out of a ploughshare, or a plough got set in the furrow and had to be cut out.

To speak literally, a hundred Irishmen, with Yankee overseers, came from Cambridge every day to get out the ice. They divided it into cakes by methods too well known to require description, and these, being sledded to the shore, were rapidly hauled off on to an ice platform, and raised by grappling irons and block and tackle, worked by horses, on to a stack, as surely as so many barrels of flour, and there placed evenly side by side, and row upon row, as if they formed the solid base of an obelisk designed to pierce the clouds. They told me that in a good day they could get out a thousand tons, which was the yield of about one acre. Deep ruts and "cradle holes" were worn in the ice, as on *terra firma*, by the passage of the sleds over the same track, and the horses invariably ate their oats out of cakes of ice hollowed out like buckets. They stacked up the cakes thus in the open air in a pile thirty-five feet high on one side and six or seven rods square, putting hay between the outside layers to exclude the air; for when the wind, though never so cold, finds a passage through, it will wear large cavities, leaving slight supports or studs only here and there, and finally topple it down. At first it looked like a vast blue fort or Valhalla; but when they began to tuck the coarse meadow hay into the crevices, and this became covered with rime and icicles, it looked like a venerable moss-grown and hoary ruin, built of azure-tinted marble, the abode of Winter, that old man we see in the almanac,—his shanty, as if he had a design to estivate with us. They calculated that not twenty-five per cent of this would reach its destination, and that two or three per cent would be wasted in the cars. However, a still greater part of this heap had a different destiny from what was intended; for, either because the ice was found not to keep so well as was expected, containing more air than usual, or for some other reason, it never got to market. This heap, made in the winter of '46–7 and estimated to contain ten thousand tons, was finally covered with hay and boards; and though it was unroofed the following July, and a part of it carried off, the rest remaining exposed to the sun, it stood over that summer and the next winter, and was not quite melted till September 1848. Thus the pond recovered the greater part.

Like the water, the Walden ice, seen near at hand, has a green tint, but at a distance is beautifully blue, and you can easily tell it from the white ice of the river, or the merely greenish ice of some ponds, a quarter of a mile off. Sometimes one of those great cakes slips from the ice-man's sled into the village street, and lies there for a week like a great emerald, an object of interest to all passers. I have noticed that a portion of Walden which in the state of water was green will often, when frozen, appear from the same point of view blue. So the hollows about this pond will, sometimes, in the winter, be filled with a greenish water somewhat like its own, but the next day will have frozen blue. Perhaps the blue color of water and ice is due to the light and air they contain, and the most transparent is the bluest. Ice is an interesting subject for contemplation. They told me that they had some in the ice-houses at Fresh Pond five years old which was as good as ever. Why is it that a bucket of water soon becomes putrid, but frozen remains sweet forever? It is commonly said that this is the difference between the affections and the intellect.

Thus for sixteen days I saw from my window a hundred men at work like busy husbandmen, with teams and horses and apparently all the implements of farming, such a picture as we see on the first page of the almanac; and as often as I looked out I was reminded of the fable of the lark and the reapers, or the parable of the sower, and the like; and now they are all gone, and in thirty days more, probably, I shall look from the same window on the pure sea-green Walden water there, reflecting the clouds and the trees, and sending up its evaporations in solitude, and no traces will appear that a man has ever stood there. Perhaps I shall hear a solitary loon laugh as he dives and plumes himself, or shall see a lonely fisher in his boat, like a floating leaf, beholding his form reflected in the waves, where lately a hundred men securely labored.

Thus it appears that the sweltering inhabitants of Charleston and New Orleans, of Madras and Bombay and Calcutta, drink at my well. In the morning I bathe my intellect in the stupendous and cosmogonal philosophy of the Bhagvat Geeta, since whose composition years of the gods have elapsed, and in comparison with which our modern world and its literature seem puny and trivial; and I doubt if that philosophy is not to be referred to a previous state of existence, so remote is its sublimity from our conceptions. I lay down the book and go to my well for water, and lo! there I meet the servant of the Bramin, priest of Brahma and Vishnu and Indra, who still sits in his temple on the Ganges reading the Vedas, or dwells at the root of a tree with his crust and water jug. I meet his servant come to draw water for his master, and our buckets as it were grate together in the same well. The pure Walden water is mingled with the sacred water of the Ganges. With favoring winds it is wafted past the site of the fabulous islands of Atlantis and the Hesperides, makes the periplus of Hanno, and, floating by Ternate and Tidore and the mouth of the Persian Gulf, melts in the tropic gales of the Indian seas, and is landed in ports of which Alexander only heard the names.

XVII
Spring

The opening of large tracts by the ice-cutters commonly causes a pond to break up earlier; for the water, agitated by the wind, even in cold weather, wears away the surrounding ice. But such was not the effect on Walden that year, for she had soon got a thick new garment to take the place of the old. This pond never breaks up so soon as the others in this neighborhood, on account both of its greater depth and it's having no stream passing through it to melt or wear away the ice. I never knew it to open in the course of a winter, not excepting that of '52–3, which gave the ponds so severe a trial. It commonly opens about the first of April, a week or ten days later than Flint's Pond and Fair-Haven, beginning to melt on the north side and in the shallower parts where it began to freeze. It indicates better than any water hereabouts the absolute progress of the season, being least affected by transient changes of temperature. A severe cold of a few days' duration in March may very much retard the opening of the former ponds, while the temperature of Walden increases almost uninterruptedly. A thermometer thrust into the middle of Walden on the 6th of March 1847, stood at 32°, or freezing point; near the shore at 33°; in the middle of Flint's Pond, the same day, at 32½°; at a dozen rods from the shore, in shallow water, under ice a foot thick, at 36°. This difference of three and a half degrees between the temperature of the deep water and the shallow in the latter pond, and the fact that a great proportion of it is comparatively shallow, show why it should break up so much sooner than Walden. The ice in the shallowest part was at this time several inches thinner than in the middle. In mid-winter the middle had been the warmest and the ice thinnest there. So, also, everyone who has waded about the shores of the pond in summer must have perceived how much warmer the water is close to the shore, where only three or four inches deep, than a little distance out, and on the surface where it is deep, than near the bottom. In spring the sun not only exerts an influence through the increased temperature of the air and earth, but its heat passes through ice a foot or more thick, and is reflected from the bottom in shallow water, and so also warms the water and melts the underside of the ice, at the same time that it is melting it more directly above, making it uneven, and causing the air bubbles which it contains to extend themselves upward and downward until it is completely honeycombed, and at last disappears suddenly in a single spring rain. Ice has its grain as well as wood, and when a cake begins to rot or "comb," that is, assume the appearance of honeycomb, whatever may be its position, the air cells are at right angles with what was the water surface. Where there is a rock or a log rising near to the surface the ice over it is much thinner, and is frequently quite dissolved by this reflected heat; and I have been told that in the experiment at Cambridge to freeze water in a shallow wooden pond, though the cold air circulated underneath, and so had access to both sides, the reflection of the sun from the bottom more than counterbalanced this advantage. When a warm rain in the middle of the winter melts off the snow-ice from Walden and leaves a hard dark or transparent ice on the middle, there will be a strip of rotten though thicker white ice, a rod or more wide, about the shores, created by this reflected heat. Also, as I have said, the bubbles themselves within the ice operate as burning glasses to melt the ice beneath.

The phenomena of the year take place every day in a pond on a small scale. Every morning, generally speaking, the shallow water is being warmed more rapidly than the deep, though it may not be made so warm after all, and every evening it is being cooled more rapidly until the morning. The day is an epitome of the year. The night is the winter, the morning and evening are the spring and fall, and the noon is the summer. The cracking and booming of the ice indicate a change of temperature. One pleasant morning after a cold night, February 24th, 1850, having gone to Flint's Pond to spend the day, I noticed with surprise, that when I struck the ice with the head of my axe, it resounded like a gong for many rods around, or as if I had struck on a tight drum-head. The pond began to boom about an hour after sunrise, when it felt the influence of the sun's rays slanted upon it from over the hills; it stretched itself and yawned like a waking man with a gradually increasing tumult, which was kept up three or four hours. It took a short siesta at noon, and boomed once more toward night, as the sun was withdrawing his influence. In the right stage of the weather a pond fires its evening gun with great regularity. But in the middle of the day, being full of cracks, and the air also being less elastic, it had completely lost its resonance and probably fishes and muskrats could not then have been stunned by a blow on it. The fishermen say that the "thundering of the pond" scares the fishes and prevents their biting. The pond does not thunder every evening, and I cannot tell surely when to expect its thundering; but though I may perceive no difference in the weather, it does. Who would have suspected so large and cold and thick-skinned a thing to be so sensitive? Yet it has its law to which it thunders obedience when it should as surely as the buds expand in the spring. The earth is all alive and covered with papillæ. The largest pond is as sensitive to atmospheric changes as the globule of mercury in its tube.

* * *

One attraction in coming to the woods to live was that I should have leisure and opportunity to see the spring come in. The ice in the pond at length begins to be honey-combed, and I can set my heel in it as I walk. Fogs and rains and warmer suns are gradually melting the snow; the days have grown sensibly longer; and I see how I shall get through the winter without adding to my woodpile, for large fires are no longer necessary. I am on the alert for the first signs of spring, to hear the chance note of some arriving bird, or the striped squirrel's chirp, for his stores must be now nearly exhausted, or see the woodchuck venture out of his winter quarters. On the 13th of March, after I had heard the bluebird, song-sparrow, and red-wing, the ice was still nearly a foot thick. As the weather grew warmer it was not sensibly worn away by the water, nor broken up and floated off as in rivers, but, though it was completely melted for half a rod in width about the shore, the middle was merely honey-combed and saturated with water, so that you could put your foot through it when six inches thick; but by the next day evening, perhaps, after a warm rain followed by fog, it would have wholly disappeared, all gone off with the fog, spirited away. One year I went across the middle only five days before it disappeared entirely. In 1845 Walden was first completely open on the 1st of April; in '46, the 25th of March; in '47, the 8th of April; in '51, the 28th of March; in '52, the 18th of April; in '53, the 23rd of March; in '54, about the 7th of April.

Every incident connected with the breaking up of the rivers and ponds and the settling of the weather is particularly interesting to us who live in a climate of so great extremes. When the warmer days come, they who dwell near the river hear the ice crack at night with a startling whoop as loud as artillery, as if its icy fetters were rent from end to end, and within a few days see it rapidly going out. So, the alligator comes out of the mud with quakings of the earth. One old man, who has been a close observer of Nature, and seems as thoroughly wise in regard to all her operations as if she had been put upon the stocks when he was a boy, and he had helped to lay her keel,—who has come to his growth, and can hardly acquire more of natural lore if he should live to the age of Methuselah,—told me, and I was surprised to hear him express wonder at any of Nature's operations, for I thought that there were no secrets between them, that one spring day he took his gun and boat, and thought that he would have a little sport with the ducks. There was ice still on the meadows, but it was all gone out of the river, and he dropped down without obstruction from Sudbury, where he lived, to Fair-Haven Pond, which he found, unexpectedly, covered for the most part with a firm field of ice. It was a warm day, and he was surprised to see so great a body of ice remaining. Not seeing any ducks, he hid his boat on the north or back side of an island in the pond and then concealed himself in the bushes on the south side, to await them. The ice was melted for three or four rods from the shore, and there was a smooth and warm sheet of water, with a muddy bottom, such as the ducks love, within, and he thought it likely that some would be along pretty soon. After he had lain still there about an hour he heard a low and seemingly very distant sound, but singularly grand and impressive, unlike anything he had ever heard, gradually swelling and increasing as if it would have a universal and memorable ending, a sullen rush and roar, which seemed to him all at once like the sound of a vast body of fowl coming in to settle there, and, seizing his gun, he started up in haste and excited; but he found, to his surprise, that the whole body of the ice had started while he lay there, and drifted in to the shore, and the sound he had heard was made by its edge grating on the shore,—at first gently nibbled and crumbled off, but at length heaving up and scattering its wrecks along the island to a considerable height before it came to a standstill.

At length the sun's rays have attained the right angle, and warm winds blow up mist and rain and melt the snow banks, and the sun dispersing the mist smiles on a checkered landscape of russet and white smoking with incense, through which the traveller picks his way from islet to islet, cheered by the music of a thousand tinkling rills and rivulets whose veins are filled with the blood of winter which they are bearing off.

Few phenomena gave me more delight than to observe the forms which thawing sand and clay assume in flowing down the sides of a deep cut on the railroad through which I passed on my way to the village, a phenomenon not very common on so large a scale, though the number of freshly exposed banks of the right material must have been greatly multiplied since railroads were invented. The material was sand of every degree of fineness and of various rich colors, commonly mixed with a little clay. When the frost comes out in the spring, and even in a thawing day in the winter, the sand begins to flow down the slopes like lava, sometimes bursting out through the snow and overflowing it where no sand was to be seen before. Innumerable little streams overlap and interlace one with another, exhibiting a sort of hybrid product, which obeys halfway the law of currents, and halfway that of vegetation. As it flows it takes the forms of sappy leaves or vines, making heaps of pulpy sprays a foot or more in depth, and resembling, as you look down on them, the laciniated, lobed, and imbricated thalluses of some lichens; or you are reminded of coral, of leopard's paws or birds' feet, of brains or lungs or bowels, and excrements of all kinds. It is a truly *grotesque* vegetation, whose forms and color we see imitated in bronze, a sort of architectural foliage more ancient and typical than acanthus, chiccory, ivy, vine, or any vegetable leaves; destined perhaps, under some circumstances, to become a puzzle to future geologists. The whole cut impressed me as if it were a cave with its stalactites laid open to the light. The various shades of the sand are singularly rich and agreeable, embracing the different iron colors, brown, gray, yellowish, and reddish. When the flowing mass reaches the drain at the foot of the bank it spreads out flatter into *strands*, the separate streams losing their semi-cylindrical form and gradually becoming more flat and broad, running together as they are more moist, till they form an almost flat *sand*, still variously and beautifully shaded, but in which you can trace the original forms of vegetation; till at length, in the water itself, they are converted into *banks*, like those formed off the mouths of rivers, and the forms of vegetation are lost in the ripple marks on the bottom.

The whole bank, which is from twenty to forty feet high, is sometimes overlaid with a mass of this kind of foliage, or sandy rupture, for a quarter of a mile on one or both sides, the produce of one spring day. What makes this sand foliage remarkable is its springing into existence thus suddenly. When I see on the one side the inert bank,—for the sun acts on one side first,—and on the other this luxuriant foliage, the creation of an hour, I am affected as if in a peculiar sense I stood in the laboratory of the Artist who made the world and me,—had come to where he was still at work, sporting on this bank, and with excess of energy strewing his fresh designs about. I feel as if I were nearer to the vitals of the globe, for this sandy overflow is something such a foliaceous mass as the vitals of the animal body. You find thus in the very sands an anticipation of the vegetable leaf. No wonder that the earth expresses itself outwardly in leaves, it so labors with the idea inwardly. The atoms have already learned this law and are pregnant by it. The overhanging leaf sees here its prototype. *Internally*, whether in the globe or animal body, it is a moist thick *lobe*, a word especially applicable to the liver and lungs and the *leaves* of fat, (*λειβω*, *labor*, *lapsus*, to flow or slip downward, a lapsing; λοβος, *globus*, lobe, globe; also lap, flap, and many other words,) *externally* a dry thin *leaf*, even as the *f* and *v* are a pressed and dried *b*. The radicals of *lobe* are *lb*, the soft mass of the *b* (single lobed, or B, double lobed,) with the liquid *l* behind it pressing it forward. In globe, *glb*, the guttural *g* adds to the meaning the capacity of the throat. The feathers and wings of birds are still drier and thinner leaves. Thus, also, you pass from the lumpish grub in the earth to the airy and fluttering butterfly. The very globe continually transcends and translates itself and becomes winged in its orbit. Even ice begins with delicate crystal leaves, as if it had flowed into moulds which the fronds of water plants have impressed on the watery mirror. The whole tree itself is but one leaf, and rivers are still vaster leaves whose pulp is intervening earth, and towns and cities are the ova of insects in their axils.

When the sun withdraws the sand ceases to flow, but in the morning the streams will start once more and branch and branch again into a myriad of others. You here see perchance how blood vessels are formed. If you look closely you observe that first there pushes forward from the thawing mass a stream of softened sand with a drop-like point, like the ball of the finger, feeling its way slowly and blindly downward, until at last with more heat and moisture, as the sun gets higher, the most fluid portion, in its effort to obey the law to which the most inert also yields, separates from the latter and forms for itself a meandering channel or artery within that, in which is seen a little silvery stream glancing like lightning from one stage of pulpy leaves or branches to another, and ever and anon swallowed up in the sand. It is wonderful how rapidly yet perfectly the sand organizes itself as it flows, using the best material its mass affords to form the sharp edges of its channel. Such are the sources of rivers. In the silicious matter which the water deposits is perhaps the bony system, and in the still finer soil and organic matter the fleshy fibre or cellular tissue. What is man but a mass of thawing clay? The ball of the human finger is but a drop congealed. The fingers and toes flow to their extent from the thawing mass of the body. Who knows what the human body would expand and flow out to under a more genial heaven? Is not the hand a spreading *palm* leaf with its lobes and veins? The ear may be regarded, fancifully, as a lichen, *umbilicaria*, on the side of the head, with its lobe or drop. The lip—*labium*, from *labor* (?)—laps or lapses from the sides of the cavernous mouth. The nose is a manifest congealed drop or stalactite. The chin is a still larger drop, the confluent dripping of the face. The cheeks are a slide from the brows into the valley of the face, opposed and diffused by the cheek bones. Each rounded lobe of the vegetable leaf, too, is a thick and now loitering drop, larger or smaller; the lobes are the fingers of the leaf; and as many lobes as it has, in so many directions it tends to flow, and more heat or other genial influences would have caused it to flow yet farther.

Thus, it seemed that this one hillside illustrated the principle of all the operations of Nature. The Maker of this earth but patented a leaf. What Champollion will decipher this hieroglyphic for us, that we may turn over a new leaf at last? This phenomenon is more exhilarating to me than the luxuriance and fertility of vineyards. True, it is somewhat excrementitious in its character, and there is no end to the heaps of liver lights and bowels, as if the globe were turned wrong side outward; but this suggests at least that Nature has some bowels, and there again is mother of humanity. This is the frost coming out of the ground; this is Spring. It precedes the green and flowery spring, as mythology precedes regular poetry. I know of nothing more purgative of winter fumes and indigestions. It convinces me that Earth is still in her swaddling clothes and stretches forth baby fingers on every side. Fresh curls spring from the baldest brow. There is nothing inorganic. These foliaceous heaps lie along the bank like the slag of a furnace, showing that Nature is "in full blast" within. The earth is not a mere fragment of dead history, stratum upon stratum like the leaves of a book, to be studied by geologists and antiquaries chiefly, but living poetry like the leaves of a tree, which precede flowers and fruit,—not a fossil earth, but a living earth; compared with whose great central life all animal and vegetable life is merely parasitic. Its throes will heave our exuviæ from their graves. You may melt your metals and cast them into the most beautiful moulds you can; they will never excite me like the forms which this molten earth flows out into. And not only it, but the institutions upon it, are plastic like clay in the hands of the potter.

* * *

Ere long, not only on these banks, but on every hill and plain and in every hollow, the frost comes out of the ground like a dormant quadruped from its burrow, and seeks the sea with music, or migrates to other climes in clouds. Thaw with his gentle persuasion is more powerful than Thor with his hammer. The one melts, the other but breaks in pieces.

When the ground was partially bare of snow, and a few warm days had dried its surface somewhat, it was pleasant to compare the first tender signs of the infant year just peeping forth with the stately beauty of the withered vegetation which had withstood the winter,—life-everlasting, golden-rods, pinweeds, and graceful wild grasses, more obvious and interesting frequently than in summer even, as if their beauty was not ripe till then; even cotton-grass, cat-tails, mulleins, johnswort, hard-hack, meadow-sweet, and other strong stemmed plants, those unexhausted granaries which entertain the earliest birds,—decent weeds, at least, which widowed Nature wears. I am particularly attracted by the arching and sheaf-like top of the wool-grass; it brings back the summer to our winter memories, and is among the forms which art loves to copy, and which, in the vegetable kingdom, have the same relation to types already in the mind of man that astronomy has. It is an antique style older than Greek or Egyptian. Many of the phenomena of Winter are suggestive of an inexpressible tenderness and fragile delicacy. We are accustomed to hear this king described as a rude and boisterous tyrant; but with the gentleness of a lover, he adorns the tresses of Summer.

At the approach of spring the red-squirrels got under my house, two at a time, directly under my feet as I sat reading or writing, and kept up the queerest chuckling and chirruping and vocal pirouetting and gurgling sounds that ever were heard; and when I stamped they only chirruped the louder, as if past all fear and respect in their mad pranks, defying humanity to stop them. No you don't—chickaree—chickaree. They were wholly deaf to my arguments, or failed to perceive their force, and fell into a strain of invective that was irresistible.

The first sparrow of spring! The year beginning with younger hope than ever! The faint silvery warblings heard over the partially bare and moist fields from the bluebird, the song-sparrow, and the red-wing, as if the last flakes of winter tinkled as they fell! What at such a time are histories, chronologies, traditions, and all written revelations? The brooks sing carols and glees to the spring. The marsh-hawk sailing low over the meadow is already seeking the first slimy life that awakes. The sinking sound of melting snow is heard in all dells, and the ice dissolves apace in the ponds. The grass flames up on the hillsides like a spring fire,—"et primitus oritur herba imbribus primoribus evocata,"—as if the earth sent forth an inward heat to greet the returning sun; not yellow but green is the color of its flame;—the symbol of perpetual youth, the grass-blade, like a long green ribbon, streams from the sod into the summer, checked indeed by the frost, but anon pushing on again, lifting its spear of last year's hay with the fresh life below. It grows as steadily as the rill oozes out of the ground. It is almost identical with that, for in the growing days of June, when the rills are dry, the grass blades are their channels, and from year to year the herds drink at this perennial green stream, and the mower draws from it betimes their winter supply. So, our human life but dies down to its root, and still puts forth its green blade to eternity.

Walden is melting apace. There is a canal two rods wide along the northerly and westerly sides, and wider still at the east end. A great field of ice has cracked off from the main body. I hear a song-sparrow singing from the bushes on the shore, *—olit, olit, olit, —chip, chip, chip, che char, —che wiss, wiss, wiss.* He too is helping to crack it. How handsome the great sweeping curves in the edge of the ice, answering somewhat to those of the shore, but more regular! It is unusually hard, owing to the recent severe but transient cold, and all watered or waved like a palace floor. But the wind slides eastward over its opaque surface in vain, till it reaches the living surface beyond. It is glorious to behold this ribbon of water sparkling in the sun, the bare face of the pond full of glee and youth, as if it spoke the joy of the fishes within it, and of the sands on its shore, a silvery sheen as from the scales of a *leuciscus*, as it were all one active fish. Such is the contrast between winter and spring. Walden was dead and is alive again. But this spring it broke up more steadily, as I have said.

The change from storm and winter to serene and mild weather, from dark and sluggish hours to bright and elastic ones, is a memorable crisis which all things proclaim. It is seemingly instantaneous at last. Suddenly an influx of light filled my house, though the evening was at hand, and the clouds of winter still overhung it, and the eaves were dripping with sleety rain. I looked out the window, and lo! where yesterday was cold gray ice there lay the transparent pond already calm and full of hope as in a summer evening, reflecting a summer evening sky in its bosom, though none was visible overhead, as if it had intelligence with some remote horizon. I heard a robin in the distance, the first I had heard for many a thousand years, methought, whose note I shall not forget for many a thousand more, the same sweet and powerful song as of yore. O the evening robin, at the end of a New England summer day! If I could ever find the twig he sits upon! I mean *he*; I mean *the twig*. This at least is not the *Turdus migratorius*. The pitch-pines and shrub-oaks about my house, which had so long drooped, suddenly resumed their several characters, looked brighter, greener, and more erect and alive, as if effectually cleansed and restored by the rain. I knew that it would not rain any more. You may tell by looking at any twig of the forest, ay, at your very woodpile, whether its winter is past or not. As it grew darker, I was startled by the *honking* of geese flying low over the woods, like weary travellers getting in late from southern lakes, and indulging at last in unrestrained complaint and mutual consolation. Standing at my door, I could hear the rush of their wings; when, driving toward my house, they suddenly spied my light, and with hushed clamor wheeled and settled in the pond. So, I came in, and shut the door, and passed my first spring night in the woods.

In the morning, I watched the geese from the door through the mist, sailing in the middle of the pond, fifty rods off, so large and tumultuous that Walden appeared like an artificial pond for their amusement. But when I stood on the shore, they at once rose up with a great flapping of wings at the signal of their commander, and when they had got into rank circled about over my head, twenty-nine of them, and then steered straight to Canada, with a regular *honk* from the leader at intervals, trusting to break their fast in muddier pools. A "plump" of ducks rose at the same time and took the route to the north in the wake of their noisier cousins.

For a week I heard the circling, groping clangor of some solitary goose in the foggy mornings, seeking its companion, and still peopling the woods with the sound of a larger life than they could sustain. In April the pigeons were seen again flying express in small flocks, and in due time I heard the martins twittering over my clearing, though it had not seemed that the township contained so many that it could afford me any, and I fancied that they were peculiarly of the ancient race that dwelt in hollow trees ere white men came. In almost all climes the tortoise and the frog are among the precursors and heralds of this season, and birds fly with song and glancing plumage, and plants spring and bloom, and winds blow, to correct this slight oscillation of the poles and preserve the equilibrium of Nature.

As every season seems best to us in its turn, so the coming in of spring is like the creation of Cosmos out of Chaos and the realization of the Golden Age.

"Eurus ad Auroram Nabathæaque regna recessit,
Persidaque, et radiis juga subdita matutinis."

"The East-Wind withdrew to Aurora and the Nabathæan kingdom,
And the Persian, and the ridges placed under the morning rays

* * * *

Man was born. Whether that Artificer of things,
The origin of a better world, made him from the divine seed;
Or the earth, being recent and lately sundered from the high
Ether, retained some seeds of cognate heaven."

A single gentle rain makes the grass many shades greener. So, our prospects brighten on the influx of better thoughts. We should be blessed if we lived in the present always, and took advantage of every accident that befell us, like the grass which confesses the influence of the slightest dew that falls on it; and did not spend our time in atoning for the neglect of past opportunities, which we call doing our duty. We loiter in winter while it is already spring. In a pleasant spring morning, all men's sins are forgiven. Such a day is a truce to vice. While such a sun holds out to burn, the vilest sinner may return. Through our own recovered innocence we discern the innocence of our neighbors. You may have known your neighbor yesterday for a thief, a drunkard, or a sensualist, and merely pitied or despised him, and despaired of the world; but the sun shines bright and warm this first spring morning, re-creating the world, and you meet him at some serene work, and see how his exhausted and debauched veins expand with still joy and bless the new day, feel the spring influence with the innocence of infancy, and all his faults are forgotten. There is not only an atmosphere of goodwill about him, but even a savor of holiness groping for expression, blindly and ineffectually perhaps, like a new-born instinct, and for a short hour the south hillside echoes to no vulgar jest. You see some innocent fair shoots preparing to burst from his gnarled rind and try another year's life, tender and fresh as the youngest plant. Even he has entered into the joy of his Lord. Why the jailer does not leave open his prison doors, —why the judge does not dismiss his case, —why the preacher does not dismiss his congregation! It is because they do not obey the hint which God gives them, nor accept the pardon which he freely offers to all.

"A return to goodness produced each day in the tranquil and beneficent breath of the morning, causes that in respect to the love of virtue and the hatred of vice, one approaches a little the primitive nature of man, as the sprouts of the forest which has been felled. In like manner the evil which one does in the interval of a day prevents the germs of virtues which began to spring up again from developing themselves and destroys them.

"After the germs of virtue have thus been prevented many times from developing themselves, then the beneficent breath of evening does not suffice to preserve them. As soon as the breath of evening does not suffice longer to preserve them, then the nature of man does not differ much from that of the brute. Men seeing the nature of this man like that of the brute, think that he has never possessed the innate faculty of reason. Are those the true and natural sentiments of man?"

"The Golden Age was first created, which without any avenger
Spontaneously without law cherished fidelity and rectitude.
Punishment and fear were not; nor were threatening words read
On suspended brass; nor did the suppliant crowd fear
The words of their judge; but were safe without an avenger.
Not yet the pine felled on its mountains had descended
To the liquid waves that it might see a foreign world,
And mortals knew no shores but their own.

* * * *

There was eternal spring, and placid zephyrs with warm
Blasts soothed the flowers born without seed."

On the 29th of April, as I was fishing from the bank of the river near the Nine-Acre-Corner bridge, standing on the quaking grass and willow roots, where the muskrats lurk, I heard a singular rattling sound, somewhat like that of the sticks which boys play with their fingers, when, looking up, I observed a very slight and graceful hawk, like a night-hawk, alternately soaring like a ripple and tumbling a rod or two over and over, showing the underside of its wings, which gleamed like a satin ribbon in the sun, or like the pearly inside of a shell. This sight reminded me of falconry and what nobleness and poetry are associated with that sport. The Merlin it seemed to me it might be called: but I care not for its name. It was the most ethereal flight I had ever witnessed. It did not simply flutter like a butterfly, nor soar like the larger hawks, but it sported with proud reliance in the fields of air; mounting again and again with its strange chuckle, it repeated its free and beautiful fall, turning over and over like a kite, and then recovering from its lofty tumbling, as if it had never set its foot on *terra firma.* It appeared to have no companion in the universe, sporting there alone, and to need none but the morning and the ether with which it played. It was not lonely but made all the earth lonely beneath it. Where was the parent which hatched it, its kindred, and its father in the heavens? The tenant of the air, it seemed related to the earth but by an egg hatched sometime in the crevice of a crag; or was its native nest made in the angle of a cloud, woven of the rainbow's trimmings and the sunset sky, and lined with some soft midsummer haze caught up from earth? Its eyry now some cliffy cloud.

Beside this I got a rare mess of golden and silver and bright cupreous fishes, which looked like a string of jewels. Ah! I have penetrated to those meadows on the morning of many a first spring day, jumping from hummock to hummock, from willow root to willow root, when the wild river valley and the woods were bathed in so pure and bright a light as would have waked the dead, if they had been slumbering in their graves, as some suppose. There needs no stronger proof of immortality. All things must live in such a light. O Death, where was thy sting? O Grave, where was thy victory, then?

Our village life would stagnate if it were not for the unexplored forests and meadows which surround it. We need the tonic of wildness to wade sometimes in marshes where the bittern and the meadow-hen lurk and hear the booming of the snipe; to smell the whispering sedge where only some wilder and more solitary fowl builds her nest, and the mink crawls with its belly close to the ground. At the same time that we are earnest to explore and learn all things, we require that all things be mysterious and unexplorable, that land and sea be infinitely wild, unsurveyed and unfathomed by us because unfathomable. We can never have enough of Nature. We must be refreshed by the sight of inexhaustible vigor, vast and Titanic features, the seacoast with its wrecks, the wilderness with its living and its decaying trees, the thunder cloud, and the rain which lasts three weeks and produces freshets. We need to witness our own limits transgressed, and some life pasturing freely where we never wander. We are cheered when we observe the vulture feeding on the carrion which disgusts and disheartens us and deriving health and strength from the repast. There was a dead horse in the hollow by the path to my house, which compelled me sometimes to go out of my way, especially in the night when the air was heavy, but the assurance it gave me of the strong appetite and inviolable health of Nature was my compensation for this. I love to see that Nature is so rife with life that myriads can be afforded to be sacrificed and suffered to prey on one another; that tender organizations can be so serenely squashed out of existence like pulp, tadpoles which herons gobble up, and tortoises and toads run over in the road; and that sometimes it has rained flesh and blood! With the liability to accident, we must see how little account is to be made of it. The impression made on a wise man is that of universal innocence. Poison is not poisonous after all, nor are any wounds fatal. Compassion is a very untenable ground. It must be expeditious. Its pleadings will not bear to be stereotyped.

Early in May, the oaks, hickories, maples, and other trees, just putting out amidst the pine woods around the pond, imparted a brightness like sunshine to the landscape, especially in cloudy days, as if the sun were breaking through mists and shining faintly on the hillsides here and there. On the third or fourth of May I saw a loon in the pond, and during the first week of the month I heard the whippoorwill, the brown-thrasher, the veery, the wood-pewee, the chewink, and other birds. I had heard the wood-thrush long before. The phœbe had already come once more and looked in at my door and window, to see if my house was cavern-like enough for her, sustaining herself on humming wings with clinched talons, as if she held by the air, while she surveyed the premises. The sulphur-like pollen of the pitch-pine soon covered the pond and the stones and rotten wood along the shore, so that you could have collected a barrel-ful. This is the "sulphur showers" we hear of. Even in Calidas' drama of Sacontala, we read of "rills dyed yellow with the golden dust of the lotus." And so, the seasons went rolling on into summer, as one rambles into higher and higher grass.

Thus was my first year's life in the woods completed; and the second year was similar to it. I finally left Walden September 6th, 1847.

XVIII
Conclusion

To the sick the doctors wisely recommend a change of air and scenery. Thank Heaven, here is not all the world. The buckeye does not grow in New England, and the mockingbird is rarely heard here. The wild goose is more of a cosmopolite than we; he breaks his fast in Canada, takes a luncheon in the Ohio, and plumes himself for the night in a southern bayou. Even the bison, to some extent, keeps pace with the seasons, cropping the pastures of the Colorado only till a greener and sweeter grass awaits him by the Yellowstone. Yet we think that if rail-fences are pulled down, and stone walls piled up on our farms, bounds are henceforth set to our lives and our fates decided. If you are chosen town-clerk, forsooth, you cannot go to Tierra del Fuego this summer: but you may go to the land of infernal fire nevertheless. The universe is wider than our views of it.

Yet we should oftener look over the tafferel of our craft, like curious passengers, and not make the voyage like stupid sailors picking oakum. The other side of the globe is but the home of our correspondent. Our voyaging is only great-circle sailing, and the doctors prescribe for diseases of the skin merely. One hastens to Southern Africa to chase the giraffe; but surely that is not the game he would be after. How long, pray, would a man hunt giraffes if he could? Snipes and woodcocks also may afford rare sport; but I trust it would be nobler game to shoot one's self.

"Direct your eye right inward, and you'll find
A thousand regions in your mind
Yet undiscovered. Travel them, and be
Expert in home-cosmography."

What does Africa, what does the West stand for? Is not our own interior white on the chart? black though it may prove, like the coast, when discovered. Is it the source of the Nile, or the Niger, or the Mississippi, or a North-West Passage around this continent, that we would find? Are these the problems which most concern mankind? Is Franklin the only man who is lost, that his wife should be so earnest to find him? Does Mr. Grinnell know where he himself is? Be rather the Mungo Park, the Lewis and Clarke and Frobisher, of your own streams and oceans; explore your own higher latitudes, with shiploads of preserved meats to support you, if they be necessary; and pile the empty cans sky-high for a sign. Were preserved meats invented to preserve meat merely? Nay, be a Columbus to whole new continents and worlds within you, opening new channels, not of trade, but of thought. Every man is the lord of a realm beside which the earthly empire of the Czar is but a petty state, a hummock left by the ice. Yet some can be patriotic who have no *self*-respect and sacrifice the greater to the less. They love the soil which makes their graves but have no sympathy with the spirit which may still animate their clay. Patriotism is a maggot in their heads. What was the meaning of that South-Sea Exploring Expedition, with all its parade and expense, but an indirect recognition of the fact, that there are continents and seas in the moral world to which every man is an isthmus or an inlet, yet unexplored by him, but that it is easier to sail many thousand miles through cold and storm and cannibals, in a government ship, with five hundred men and boys to assist one, than it is to explore the private sea, the Atlantic and Pacific Ocean of one's being alone.

> *"Erret, et extremos alter scrutetur Iberos.*
> *Plus habet hic vitæ, plus habet ille viæ."*

> *Let them wander and scrutinize the outlandish Australians.*
> *I have more of God, they more of the road.*

It is not worth the while to go round the world to count the cats in Zanzibar. Yet do this even till you can do better, and you may perhaps find some "Symmes' Hole" by which to get at the inside at last. England and France, Spain and Portugal, Gold Coast and Slave Coast, all front on this private sea; but no bark from them has ventured out of sight of land, though it is without doubt the direct way to India. If you would learn to speak all tongues and conform to the customs of all nations, if you would travel farther than all travellers, be naturalized in all climes, and cause the Sphinx to dash her head against a stone, even obey the precept of the old philosopher, and Explore thyself. Herein are demanded the eye and the nerve. Only the defeated and deserters go to the wars, cowards that run away and enlist. Start now on that farthest western way, which does not pause at the Mississippi or the Pacific, nor conduct toward a worn-out China or Japan, but leads on direct a tangent to this sphere, summer and winter, day and night, sundown, moon down, and at last earth down too.

It is said that Mirabeau took to highway robbery "to ascertain what degree of resolution was necessary in order to place oneself in formal opposition to the most sacred laws of society." He declared that "a soldier who fights in the ranks does not require half so much courage as a foot-pad,"— "that honor and religion have never stood in the way of a well-considered and a firm resolve." This was manly, as the world goes; and yet it was idle, if not desperate. A saner man would have found himself often enough "in formal opposition" to what are deemed "the most sacred laws of society," through obedience to yet more sacred laws, and so have tested his resolution without going out of his way. It is not for a man to put himself in such an attitude to society, but to maintain himself in whatever attitude he find himself through obedience to the laws of his being, which will never be one of opposition to a just government, if he should chance to meet with such.

I left the woods for as good a reason as I went there. Perhaps it seemed to me that I had several more lives to live and could not spare any more time for that one. It is remarkable how easily and insensibly we fall into a particular route and make a beaten track for ourselves. I had not lived there a week before my feet wore a path from my door to the pond-side; and though it is five or six years since I trod it, it is still quite distinct. It is true, I fear that others may have fallen into it and so helped to keep it open. The surface of the earth is soft and impressible by the feet of men; and so with the paths which the mind travels. How worn and dusty, then, must be the highways of the world, how deep the ruts of tradition and conformity! I did not wish to take a cabin passage, but rather to go before the mast and on the deck of the world, for there I could best see the moonlight amid the mountains. I do not wish to go below now.

I learned this, at least, by my experiment; that if one advances confidently in the direction of his dreams, and endeavors to live the life which he has imagined, he will meet with a success unexpected in common hours. He will put some things behind, will pass an invisible boundary; new, universal, and more liberal laws will begin to establish themselves around and within him; or the old laws be expanded, and interpreted in his favor in a more liberal sense, and he will live with the license of a higher order of beings. In proportion as he simplifies his life, the laws of the universe will appear less complex, and solitude will not be solitude, nor poverty poverty, nor weakness weakness. If you have built castles in the air, your work need not be lost; that is where they should be. Now put the foundations under them.

It is a ridiculous demand which England and America make, that you shall speak so that they can understand you. Neither men nor toadstools grow so. As if that were important, and there were not enough to understand you without them. As if Nature could support but one order of understandings, could not sustain birds as well as quadrupeds, flying as well as creeping things, and *hush* and *who*, which Bright can understand, were the best English. As if there were safety in stupidity alone. I fear chiefly lest my expression may not be *extra-vagant* enough, may not wander far enough beyond the narrow limits of my daily experience, so as to be adequate to the truth of which I have been convinced. *Extra vagance!* it depends on how you are yarded. The migrating buffalo, which seeks new pastures in another latitude, is not extravagant like the cow which kicks over the pail, leaps the cow-yard fence, and runs after her calf, in milking time. I desire to speak somewhere *without* bounds; like a man in a waking moment, to men in their waking moments; for I am convinced that I cannot exaggerate enough even to lay the foundation of a true expression. Who that has heard a strain of music feared then lest he should speak extravagantly any more forever? In view of the future or possible, we should live quite laxly and undefined in front, our outlines dim and misty on that side as our shadows reveal an insensible perspiration toward the sun. The volatile truth of our words should continually betray the inadequacy of the residual statement. Their truth is instantly *translated*; its literal monument alone remains. The words which express our faith and piety are not definite; yet they are significant and fragrant like frankincense to superior natures.

Why level downward to our dullest perception always, and praise that as common sense? The commonest sense is the sense of men asleep, which they express by snoring. Sometimes we are inclined to class those who are once-and-a-half-witted with the half-witted, because we appreciate only a third part of their wit. Some would find fault with the morning-red, if they ever got up early enough. "They pretend," as I hear, "that the verses of Kabir have four different senses; illusion, spirit, intellect, and the exoteric doctrine of the Vedas;" but in this part of the world it is considered a ground for complaint if a man's writings admit of more than one interpretation. While England endeavors to cure the potato rot, will not any endeavor to cure the brain rot, which prevails so much more widely and fatally?

I do not suppose that I have attained to obscurity, but I should be proud if no more fatal fault were found with my pages on this score than was found with the Walden ice. Southern customers objected to its blue color, which is the evidence of its purity, as if it were muddy, and preferred the Cambridge ice, which is white, but tastes of weeds. The purity men love is like the mists which envelop the earth, and not like the azure ether beyond.

Some are dinning in our ears that we Americans, and moderns generally, are intellectual dwarfs compared with the ancients, or even the Elizabethan men. But what is that to the purpose? A living dog is better than a dead lion. Shall a man go and hang himself because he belongs to the race of pygmies, and not be the biggest pygmy that he can? Let everyone mind his own business, and endeavor to be what he was made.

Why should we be in such desperate haste to succeed, and in such desperate enterprises? If a man does not keep pace with his companions, perhaps it is because he hears a different drummer. Let him step to the music which he hears, however measured or far away. It is not important that he should mature as soon as an apple tree or an oak. Shall he turn his spring into summer? If the condition of things which we were made for is not yet, what were any reality which we can substitute? We will not be shipwrecked on a vain reality. Shall we with pains erect a heaven of blue glass over ourselves, though when it is done, we shall be sure to gaze still at the true ethereal heaven far above, as if the former were not?

There was an artist in the city of Kouroo who was disposed to strive after perfection. One day it came into his mind to make a staff. Having considered that in an imperfect work time is an ingredient, but into a perfect work time does not enter, he said to himself, It shall be perfect in all respects, though I should do nothing else in my life. He proceeded instantly to the forest for wood, being resolved that it should not be made of unsuitable material; and as he searched for and rejected stick after stick, his friends gradually deserted him, for they grew old in their works and died, but he grew not older by a moment. His singleness of purpose and resolution, and his elevated piety, endowed him, without his knowledge, with perennial youth. As he made no compromise with Time, Time kept out of his way and only sighed at a distance because he could not overcome him. Before he had found a stock in all respects suitable the city of Kouroo was a hoary ruin, and he sat on one of its mounds to peel the stick. Before he had given it the proper shape the dynasty of the Candahars was at an end, and with the point of the stick he wrote the name of the last of that race in the sand and then resumed his work. By the time he had smoothed and polished the staff Kalpa was no longer the pole-star; and ere he had put on the ferrule and the head adorned with precious stones, Brahma had awoke and slumbered many times. But why do I stay to mention these things? When the finishing stroke was put to his work, it suddenly expanded before the eyes of the astonished artist into the fairest of all the creations of Brahma. He had made a new system in making a staff, a world with full and fair proportions; in which, though the old cities and dynasties had passed away, fairer and more glorious ones had taken their places. And now he saw by the heap of shavings still fresh at his feet, that, for him and his work, the former lapse of time had been an illusion, and that no more time had elapsed than is required for a single scintillation from the brain of Brahma to fall on and inflame the tinder of a mortal brain. The material was pure, and his art was pure; how could the result be other than wonderful?

No face which we can give to a matter will stead us so well at last as the truth. This alone wears well. For the most part, we are not where we are, but in a false position. Through an infirmity of our natures, we suppose a case, and put ourselves into it, and hence are in two cases at the same time, and it is doubly difficult to get out. In sane moments we regard only the facts, the case that is. Say what you have to say, not what you ought. Any truth is better than make-believe. Tom Hyde, the tinker, standing on the gallows, was asked if he had anything to say. "Tell the tailors," said he, "to remember to make a knot in their thread before they take the first stitch." His companion's prayer is forgotten.

However mean your life is, meet it and live it; do not shun it and call it hard names. It is not so bad as you are. It looks poorest when you are richest. The fault-finder will find faults even in paradise. Love your life, poor as it is. You may perhaps have some pleasant, thrilling, glorious hours, even in a poor-house. The setting sun is reflected from the windows of the alms-house as brightly as from the rich man's abode, the snow melts before its door as early in the spring. I do not see but a quiet mind may live as contentedly there, and have as cheering thoughts, as in a palace. The town's poor seem to me often to live the most independent lives of any. Maybe they are simply great enough to receive without misgiving. Most think that they are above being supported by the town; but it oftener happens that they are not above supporting themselves by dishonest means, which should be more disreputable. Cultivate poverty like a garden herb, like sage. Do not trouble yourself much to get new things, whether clothes or friends. Turn the old; return to them. Things do not change; we change. Sell your clothes and keep your thoughts. God will see that you do not want society. If I were confined to a corner of a garret all my days, like a spider, the world would be just as large to me while I had my thoughts about me. The philosopher said: "From an army of three divisions one can take away its general and put it in disorder; from the man the most abject and vulgar one cannot take away his thought." Do not seek so anxiously to be developed, to subject yourself to many influences to be played on; it is all dissipation. Humility like darkness reveals the heavenly lights. The shadows of poverty and meanness gather around us, "and lo! creation widens to our view." We are often reminded that if there were bestowed on us the wealth of

Crœsus, our aims must still be the same, and our means essentially the same. Moreover, if you are restricted in your range by poverty, if you cannot buy books and newspapers, for instance, you are but confined to the most significant and vital experiences; you are compelled to deal with the material which yields the most sugar and the most starch. It is life near the bone where it is sweetest. You are defended from being a trifler. No man loses ever on a lower level by magnanimity on a higher. Superfluous wealth can buy superfluities only. Money is not required to buy one necessary of the soul.

I live in the angle of a leaden wall, into whose composition was poured a little alloy of bell metal. Often, in the repose of my midday, there reaches my ears a confused *tintinnabulum* from without. It is the noise of my contemporaries. My neighbors tell me of their adventures with famous gentlemen and ladies, what notabilities they met at the dinner-table; but I am no more interested in such things than in the contents of the Daily Times. The interest and the conversation are about costume and manners chiefly; but a goose is a goose still, dress it as you will. They tell me of California and Texas, of England and the Indies, of the Hon. Mr. —— of Georgia or of Massachusetts, all transient and fleeting phenomena, till I am ready to leap from their courtyard like the Mameluke bey. I delight to come to my bearings, not walk in procession with pomp and parade, in a conspicuous place, but to walk even with the Builder of the universe, if I may, not to live in this restless, nervous, bustling, trivial Nineteenth Century, but stand or sit thoughtfully while it goes by. What are men celebrating? They are all on a committee of arrangements and hourly expect a speech from somebody. God is only the president of the day, and Webster is his orator. I love to weigh, to settle, to gravitate toward that which most strongly and rightfully attracts me; not hang by the beam of the scale and try to weigh less, not suppose a case, but take the case that is; to travel the only path I can, and that on which no power can resist me. It affords me no satisfaction to commence to spring an arch before I have got a solid foundation. Let us not play at kittly-benders. There is a solid bottom everywhere. We read that the traveller asked the boy if the swamp before him had a hard bottom. The boy replied that it had. But presently the traveller's horse sank in up to the girths, and he observed to the boy, "I thought you said that this bog had a hard bottom." "So it has," answered the latter, "but you have not got halfway to it yet." So it is with the bogs and quicksands of society; but he is an old boy that knows it. Only what is thought, said, or done at a certain rare coincidence is good. I would not be one of those who will foolishly drive a nail into mere lath and plastering; such a deed would keep me awake nights. Give me a hammer and let me feel for the furring. Do not depend on the putty. Drive a nail home and clinch it so faithfully that you can wake up in the night and think of your work with satisfaction, a work at which you would not be ashamed to invoke the Muse. So will help you God, and so only. Every nail driven should be as another rivet in the machine of the universe, you carrying on the work.

Rather than love, than money, than fame, give me truth. I sat at a table where were rich food and wine in abundance, and obsequious attendance, but sincerity and truth were not; and I went away hungry from the inhospitable board. The hospitality was as cold as the ices. I thought that there was no need of ice to freeze them. They talked to me of the age of the wine and the fame of the vintage; but I thought of an older, a newer, and purer wine, of a more glorious vintage, which they had not got, and could not buy. The style, the house and grounds and "entertainment" pass for nothing with me. I called on the king, but he made me wait in his hall and conducted like a man incapacitated for hospitality. There was a man in my neighborhood who lived in a hollow tree. His manners were truly regal. I should have done better had I called on him.

How long shall we sit in our porticoes practising idle and musty virtues, which any work would make impertinent? As if one were to begin the day with long-suffering and hire a man to hoe his potatoes; and in the afternoon go forth to practise Christian meekness and charity with goodness aforethought! Consider the China pride and stagnant self-complacency of mankind. This generation inclines a little to congratulate itself on being the last of an illustrious line; and in Boston and London and Paris and Rome, thinking of its long descent, it speaks of its progress in art and science and literature with satisfaction. There are the Records of the Philosophical Societies, and the public Eulogies of *Great Men!* It is the good Adam contemplating his own virtue. "Yes, we have done great deeds, and sung divine songs, which shall never die,"—that is, as long as *we* can remember them. The learned societies and great men of Assyria, where are they? What youthful philosophers and experimentalists we are! There is not one of my readers who has yet lived a whole human life. These may be but the spring months in the life of the race. If we have had the seven-years' itch, we have not seen the seventeen-year locust yet in Concord. We are acquainted with a mere pellicle of the globe on which we live. Most have not delved six feet beneath the surface, nor leaped as many above it. We know not where we are. Beside, we are sound asleep nearly half our time. Yet we esteem ourselves wise and have an established order on the surface. Truly, we are deep thinkers, we are ambitious spirits! As I stand over the insect crawling amid the pine needles on the forest floor, and endeavoring to conceal itself from my sight, and ask myself why it will cherish those humble thoughts, and hide its head from me who might, perhaps, be its benefactor, and impart to its race some cheering information, I am reminded of the greater Benefactor and Intelligence that stands over me the human insect.

There is an incessant influx of novelty into the world, and yet we tolerate incredible dullness. I need only suggest what kind of sermons are still listened to in the most enlightened countries. There are such words as joy and sorrow, but they are only the burden of a psalm, sung with a nasal twang, while we believe in the ordinary and mean. We think that we can change our clothes only. It is said that the British Empire is very large and respectable, and that the United States are a first-rate power. We do not believe that a tide rises and falls behind every man which can float the British Empire like a chip, if he should ever harbor it in his mind. Who knows what sort of seventeen-year locust will next come out of the ground? The government of the world I live in was not framed, like that of Britain, in after-dinner conversations over the wine.

The life in us is like the water in the river. It may rise this year higher than man has ever known it and flood the parched uplands; even this may be the eventful year, which will drown out all our muskrats. It was not always dry land where we dwell. I see far inland the banks which the stream anciently washed, before science began to record its freshets. Everyone has heard the story which has gone the rounds of New England, of a strong and beautiful bug which came out of the dry leaf of an old table of apple-tree wood, which had stood in a farmer's kitchen for sixty years, first in Connecticut, and afterward in Massachusetts,—from an egg deposited in the living tree many years earlier still, as appeared by counting the annual layers beyond it; which was heard gnawing out for several weeks, hatched perchance by the heat of an urn. Who does not feel his faith in a resurrection and immortality strengthened by hearing of this? Who knows what beautiful and winged life, whose egg has been buried for ages under many concentric layers of woodenness in the dead dry life of society, deposited at first in the alburnum of the green and living tree, which has been gradually converted into the semblance of its well-seasoned tomb,—heard perchance gnawing out now for years by the astonished family of man, as they sat round the festive board,—may unexpectedly come forth from amidst society's most trivial and handselled furniture, to enjoy its perfect summer life at last!

I do not say that John or Jonathan will realize all this; but such is the character of that morrow which mere lapse of time can never make to dawn. The light which puts out our eyes is darkness to us. Only that day dawns to which we are awake. There is more day to dawn. The sun is but a morning star.

THE END

ANNE SPENCER (1882–1975)

Annie Bethel Scales Bannister (later Anne Spencer) was born on a farm in Henry County, Virginia on February 6th, 1882. Her parents, Joel Cephus Bannister and Sarah Louise Scales, were former slaves. Mr. Bannister had a mix of Black, White, and Seminole Indian ancestry. After Spencer was born, the family moved to Martinsville, Virginia. There, her father opened a saloon, but after the separation of her parents, Spencer and her mother briefly went to Bramwell, West Virginia. To be able to work and provide for the two of them, Scales put Spencer into foster care with William Dixie and his wife.

Her mother sought out formal education for Spencer rather than the segregated public schools in West Virginia, so the two moved to Lynchburg, Virginia so that Spencer could enroll in the Virginia Theological Seminary and College. Despite her mother's lie that Spencer was already twelve, Spencer started schooling for the first time at eleven years old. The school itself was a pioneering Black college that offered equal curriculum instead of teaching the bare minimum of literacy and occupational training. Spencer was barely literate when she joined the school in 1893, but at her graduation in 1899, she delivered the Valedictorian speech.

Spencer met Edward Alexander Spencer in school and the two started tutoring each other in math and languages. Edward became the first African American postal worker in Lynchburg, as well as becoming an entrepreneur in construction and business. By 1901, the two were married and moved into the Queen Anne-style home that Edward had designed and constructed himself. Spencer gave birth to three children—Bethel Calloway, Alroy Sarah, and Chauncey Edward. Edward's entrepreneurial talents and Spencer's work as a librarian helped send all three children to college. Chauncey later became an aviator who fought for greater opportunities for African American pilots.

Throughout her life, Spencer had a determination to improve the conditions of African Americans in Lynchburg. Her family hosted many Black travelers in their home since Jim Crow segregation barred African Americans from staying at local inns and hotels. Spencer and Mary Rice Hayes, the widow of the Seminary's former president, both discussed how Lynchburg needed its own NAACP branch. In 1913, their discussion became reality when Spencer, Hayes, and other community members set up the Lynchburg NAACP in Spencer's living room. James Weldon Johnson, an activist and the NAACP leader, traveled to Lynchburg to help them further establish the branch. There, Johnson discovered Spencer's talents and encouraged her to publish her writing.

Spencer's poems began showing up in magazines like *The Crisis*, *Palms*, and *Opportunity*—all associated with the Harlem Renaissance. Despite Spencer remaining in Virginia, she stayed close with many of the leading writers of the Harlem Renaissance like Langston Hughes, Zora Neale Hurston, and Countee Cullen. Her creditability through publications led her to open the first library available to Lynchburg's Black citizens in the segregated Dunbar High School in 1924. The library started with her own collection of books and Spencer was a well-loved librarian during the twenty years she worked there.

Thirty of Spencer's poems were published in her lifetime with themes of religion, race, and the natural world. With her interest in botany, she often drew inspiration from her garden and cottage her husband had built for her. Her writing allowed her to become the first African American woman to be published in the *Norton Anthology of Modern Poetry* (1973). J. Lee Greene published two dozen of her poems in his biography of Spencer, *Time's Unfading Garden: Anne Spencer's Life and Poetry* (1977).

Spencer died from cancer in 1975 and was buried next to her husband at Forest Hills Cemetery in Lynchburg. Her grandchildren run tours of her home—now the Anne Spencer House and Garden Museum—to show the original furniture, materials Edward collected on his postal route, and one of Spencer's poems, "Lines to a Nasturtium"

(1927), painted on a kitchen cabinet. Since 2019, the United States Postal Service honors Anne Spencer on a Forever Stamp in the "Harlem Renaissance" series, along with Alaine Locke, Nella Larsen, and Arturo Alfonso Schomburg.

Lines to a Nasturtium

Flame-flower, Day-torch, Mauna Loa,
I saw a daring bee, today, pause, and soar,
Into your flaming heart;
Then did I hear crisp crinkled laughter
As the furies after tore him apart?
A bird, next, small and humming,
Looked into your startled depths and fled ...
Surely, some dread sight, and dafter
Than human eyes as mine can see,
Set the stricken air waves drumming
In his flight.

Day-torch, Flame-flower, cool-hot Beauty,
I cannot see, I cannot hear your fluty
Voice lure your loving swain,
But I know one other to whom you are in beauty
Born in vain;
Hair like the setting sun,
Her eyes a rising star,
Motions gracious as reeds by Babylon, bar
All your competing;
Hands like, how like, brown lilies sweet,
Cloth of gold were fair enough to touch her feet ...
Ah, how the senses flood at my repeating,
As once in her fire-lit heart I felt the furies
Beating, beating.

White Things

Most things are colorful things—the sky, earth, and sea.
Black men are most men; but the white are free!
White things are rare things; so rare, so rare
They stole from out a silvered world—somewhere.
Finding earth-plains fair plains, save greenly grassed,
They strewed white feathers of cowardice, as they passed;
The golden stars with lances fine
The hills all red and darkened pine,
They blanched with their wand of power;
And turned the blood in a ruby rose
To a poor white poppy-flower.

They pyred a race of black, black men,
And burned them to ashes white; then
Laughing, a young one claimed a skull.
For the skull of a black is white, not dull,
But a glistening awful thing;
Made it seems, for this ghoul to swing
In the face of God with all his might,
And swear by the hell that siréd him:
"Man-maker, make white!"

Life-Long, Poor Browning...

Life-long, poor Browning never knew Virginia,
Or he'd not grieved in Florence for April sallies
Back to English gardens after Euclid's linear:
Clipt yews, Pomander Walks, and pleachéd alleys;

Primroses, prim indeed, in quite ordered hedges,
Waterways, soberly, sedately enchanneled,
No thin riotous blade even among the sedges,
All the wild country-side tamely impaneled...

Dead, now, dear Browning, lives on in heaven,—
(Heaven's Virginia when the year's at its Spring)
He's haunting the byways of the wine-aired leaven
And throating the notes of the wildings on wing;

Here canopied reaches of dogwood and hazel,
Beech tree and redbud fine-laced in vines,
Fleet clapping rills by lush fern and basil,
Drain blue hills to lowlands scented with pines...

Think you he meets in this tender green sweetness
Shade that was Elizabeth... immortal completeness!

Suggested Readings

Poetry

Coleridge, Smauel Taylor. "To Nature" (1796).

Hughes, Langston. "An Earth Song" (1925).

Hughes, Langston. "Our Land" (1923).

Keats, John. *Lamia, Isabella, The Eve of St. Agnes, and Other Poems.* Printed for Taylor and Hessey Etc., 1820.

Shelley, Percy Bysshe. "Mont Blanc" (1817).

Shelley, Percy Bysshe. "Ode to the West Wind" (1820).

Wordsworth, William. "Lines Composed a Few Miles above Tintern Abbey" (1798).

Yeats, William Butler. "The Lake Isle of Innisfree" (1890).

Prose

Bartram, William. *Travels of William Bartram.* Edited by Mark Van Doren, Dover Publications, 1955.

Cooper, Susan Fenimore. *Rural Hours.* Putnam's American Agency, 1850.

Emerson, Ralph Waldo. "Self-Reliance" (1841).

Muir, John. *A Thousand-Mile Walk to the Gulf.* Edited by William Frederic Badè, Houghton Mifflin, 1916.

Ray, John. *Flora of Cambridgeshire.* Edited by A.H. Ewen and C.T. Prime, Wheldon & Wesley Ltd, 1975.

Thoreau, Henry David. *Walden: A Fully Annotated Edition.* Edited by Jeffrey S. Cramer, Yale University Press, 2004.

Bibliography

Atkins, Jill, and Warren Maroun. "The *Naturalist's Journals* of Gilbert White: Exploring the roots of accounting for biodiversity and Extinction Accounting." *Accounting, Auditing & Accountability Journal*, vol. 33, no. 8, 4 Aug. 2020, pp. 1835–1870, https://doi.org/10.1108/aaaj-03-2016-2450.

Avery, Simon, and Rebecca Stott. *Elizabeth Barrett Browning*. Taylor & Francis Group, 2003.

Bentley, Gerald Eades. *Shakespeare: A Biographical Handbook*. Yale Uni versity Press, 1961.

Brandman, Mariana. "Biography: Anne Spencer." *National Women's History Museum*, 2021.

Ferrari, Carlyn E. "Anne Spencer's 'Natural' poetics." *CLA Journal*, vol. 61, no. 4, Sept. 2018, p. 185, https://doi.org/10.34042/claj.61.4.0185.

Harding, Walter. *The Days of Henry Thoreau: A Biography*. Dover, 1982.

Myerson, Joel, editor. *Transcendentalism: A Reader*. Oxford University Press, 2000.

Phillips, Dana. *The Truth of Ecology: Nature, Culture, and Literature in America*. Oxford University Press, 2003.

Porter, James I. *The Sublime in Antiquity*. Cambridge University Press, 2016.

Pretty, Jules N., and Sarah Pilgrim. *Nature and Culture: Rebuilding Lost Connections*. Taylor & Francis Group, 2010.

Remien, Peter. *The Concept of Nature in Early Modern English Literature*. Cambridge University Press, 2019.

Rusk, Ralph L. *The Life of Ralph Waldo Emerson*. Columbia University Press, 1949.

Scott, Charlotte. *Shakespeare's Nature: From Cultivation to Culture*. Oxford University Press, 2014.

www.ingramcontent.com/pod-product-compliance
Lightning Source LLC
Chambersburg PA
CBHW032010170626
46807CB00006B/2729